PHILIP H. HALEY

FLYING
SAFELY

FLYING SAFELY

by Richard L. Collins

Delacorte Press/Eleanor Friede

Manufactured in the United States of America

Second Printing—1978

Designed by Leonard Telesca

Library of Congress Cataloging in Publication Data
Collins, Richard L.   1933–
    Flying safely.
    Includes index.
    1. Aeronautics—Safety measures.   2. Aeronautics
—Accidents.   3. Airplanes—Piloting.   I. Title.
TL553.5.C54   629.132′5′028   77-1461
ISBN 0-440-02631-8

To my father, Leighton Collins, in appreciation for the generous footsteps he has provided for me.

Contents

Foreword

Whether it is used for business or personal reasons, the airplane offers a freedom that is unique. Slip away just for the enjoyment of flight or use the airplane as a means of transportation—either adds a rewarding new dimension to life.

There's risk with any reward, and aviation offers no exception to this rule. The nature of the activity suggests more risk than might be found in other things. We fly high and fast; any accidental stop is likely to be serious. Safety is our most important question.

Despite its importance, it is often tempting to dismiss any aviation safety problem as one involving only unintelligent pilots. Most accidents are, after all, attributed to pilot error. This is an oversimplification; pilots do not fail on purpose.

In the real world, pilots fail because they try to extract more utility or performance from an airplane than is available, or available with their level of skill. And more often than not, they do it because the risks are not understood.

We have to acknowledge, too, that the motivation to fly is oriented almost entirely toward the reward. People fly airplanes for what they do and what they offer. True, we react negatively when flying appears not to be safe, but safety is not the reason we fly.

Fear, the thing that protects us in many other situations, often makes its suggestion too late in an airplane. Many a pilot has flown the last mile concerned not with aeronautical risk, but with thoughts of being late or missing an appointment. Flying safely must thus become a second-nature, first-priority part of the action, based on understanding.

The purpose of this book is to explore accident causes and to promote an understanding of the factors that affect the general safety record. We'll see that while there will always be some risk in flying, as in any form of transportation, it can easily be minimized.

RICHARD L. COLLINS

FLYING SAFELY

1 | VFR Weather-Related Accidents

Gravity might be the most basic natural foe of the airplane, but weather is the most persistent victor over the airplane as pilots challenge nature with their mechanical birds. This is true regardless of the machine's sophistication or the pilot's level of skill. When air carriers have spectacular accidents, they almost always happen in bad weather. In fact, all the airlines would have a virtually perfect safety record if they flew only on clear days; they would also have no business after a few months of such an operation. This tells us that the risk in flying must increase as the ceiling and visibility decrease. This is the first and perhaps the most important thing a pilot must understand when starting to balance safety and utility in general aviation airplanes. The challenge is to fly as much weather as

1

possible while at the same time minimizing the risk. This book's coverage of weather is directly related only to accident causes. The nature of weather and how to interpret it is another subject.

The Typical Accident

A pilot has to crawl before walking, and VFR flying might be characterized as the crawling phase. There is no way to get places very rapidly in VFR conditions unless the weather is excellent or unless you take a lot of chances. The risk of an accident increases as the square of chances taken, so a pilot who runs scud VFR, taking several chances a minute, is enjoying the highest-risk form of weather flying. The results are predictable, so predictable that the National Transportation Safety Board (NTSB) was able to publish a report that outlined a "typical" accident. The pilot had a private certificate, between 100 and 300 hours, and crashed in rain and fog. The pilot continued VFR into adverse weather conditions on a flight being conducted for pleasure or personal transportation. This "typical" accident is a prime safety problem in general aviation.

Things haven't changed much in years, because the first weather-related accident that I remember occurred twenty-three years ago and fit the current average. This happened in the early fifties, when aviation wasn't nearly as formal as it is today. Instrument flying was not widely done, and many of those who flew weather did so through a combination of clandestine instrument flying and scud running. Most of this was self-taught, and the pilot with an Ercoupe in our hangar appeared serious about educating himself on weather flying. He outfitted the airplane with a manually rotatable loop for the low-frequency radio and added primary instruments, a turn-and-bank and vertical speed, to his panel. He talked quite a bit about the radio-navigation and instrument-flying ability he was developing, but I suppose the rest of us didn't pay much attention.

One rainy morning when we came to work at the airport, the Ercoupe was gone. It didn't return that evening, and the pilot's family became alarmed. We paid attention then. Nobody seemed to know where he had gone, and a check of his acquaintances in other communities yielded no clue. The weather improved the next day, and a search was launched.

Late in the afternoon, word came that the airplane had been spotted. A group of us were on the ground at the time and drove to join the party that was going to the site, about forty miles from the airport. We got there after dark, as they were removing the pilot from his shattered Ercoupe. It was an impressive sight. I had been flying for a couple of years, but until that instant I don't suppose I was completely convinced that airplanes could bite.

We went back the next day to watch the investigation. Most of the airplane was in one spot, but some fabric and parts from one wing were strewn through the woods in the direction from which the airplane came as the flight terminated. A nearby witness said a small airplane had flown over low and that one wing appeared to be "flapping."

The events leading to the accident started fitting into

place. He crashed near a river bottom, and all of us knew from experience that the ceiling and visibility over the bottom land was always lower than elsewhere. General conditions at reporting stations the morning of the accident had been around 500 overcast with two miles visibility in rain and fog. Clouds were probably in the treetops as the pilot flew into this area. What next? The pilot apparently pulled up, into the clouds. Nobody knows for sure what his plan was, but perhaps he intended to fly instruments for a while and then attempt a letdown. At this stage, the risk involved probably wasn't apparent, and the pilot probably was not frightened. In fact, he could have had a rather methodical plan in mind for pressing on. But his self-taught ability to fly instruments was not adequate. Control was eventually lost, and the airplane was overstressed, resulting in the failure of a wing. It was a classic case of a pilot continuing VFR into adverse weather conditions and losing control.

The Need to "Be There" on Time

The pilot's mistake in continuing on into poor weather, instead of retreating, is as typical today as it was in the fifties. This part of the sequence leading to a weather-related accident might be called the first stage.

To begin, why press on VFR, into the shadow of cloud and possible disaster? The search for utility is a leading reason. In this incident the pilot wanted to make the Ercoupe work for him, to take him to a destination on schedule even though the weather was not good. There is probably an urgent compulsion to be somewhere behind virtually all weather-related accidents. Whether it be a need to get back home Sunday night for work on Monday, to "be there" for a big business deal, to get to a football game, to arrive on time for a clandestine meeting with a lover, or whatever, there's pride in being on time and at least imagined loss of face in canceling.

One key to risk management is to forget any attempt at scheduling arrivals on a VFR basis; weather is too fickle for a VFR pilot to say he's going to arrive anywhere at 8:oo A.M. next Tuesday. Another key is a continuing reevaluation of reasons for continuing once en route. If the continuation is related to business or pleasure, instead of the view ahead, the pilot has completely moved from the risk-management business to a reliance on luck, a very unreliable aeronautical commodity. It is often difficult to do, but the airplane and its environment must be mentally separated from all other considerations. There's just no way to allow the importance of a trip to influence the go/no-go decision without inviting trouble.

Training

There are certainly considerations other than pressure to "be there" involved in VFR weather-related accidents. The training system has made a strong contribution to weather accidents by steadfastly refusing, over the years, to recognize the need for dual cross-country in marginal weather conditions. A lot of newly licensed private pilots probably fly on into instrument conditions simply because they do not know the visual appearance of the impossible. There is no way to learn the hazards of poking around in scud without doing it. Purists say that a pilot without instrument training should stay away from all clouds, that those who get close to clouds are breaking the law, and that this simple solution solves the total problem. True, in an idealistic sense, but every pilot is going to take a bite of the apple, and every pilot should thus be aware of the things that might bite back.

Being able to sample is one great advantage the airplane has over the automobile. An instructor can fly into marginal weather, get ice on the wings, shut engines off, stall, spin, and do all manner of terrible things with student pilots to show them the flaky side of the business. And these can all be done safely in carefully selected conditions. When I first taught our daughter to drive, I was a little taken by the fact that I couldn't demonstrate a blowout, a skid, or any of the bad things that happen in cars without donating one car to each demonstration. The hazards of marginal VFR can be safely demonstrated to students and they should be demonstrated. A school that gives dual cross-country only on clear days is simply not giving new pilots the tools necessary to make educated decisions on when to continue and when not to continue.

Weather Information

Weather information, and the way pilots consider it, is another integral part of the initial phase of continuing VFR into weather trouble. The time-honored system of checking the forecasts and the sequences is socially acceptable but rather ineffective. A good example of the hazards of such a procedure is found in western Arkansas and eastern Oklahoma. There is a notorious mountain there, Rich Mountain, that has been assaulted by a virtual squadron of airline, military, and general aviation aircraft over the years. (They haven't all actually hit Rich Mountain; some have used other mountains in the area.) The nearest airport weather-reporting stations are Fort Smith, Hot Springs, and Texarkana in Arkansas and McAlester, Oklahoma. It is quite common for all these stations to report good VFR and for Rich Mountain and its compatriots to be in the clouds. Many don't realize the hills are high in the area, and many pilots thus fly complacently (aided by a vortac on top of the mountain) into the area when the weather is bad and the ridges are obscured.

The FAA and the National Weather Service worked out a plan to put an automatic weather station atop Rich Mountain; this should help spread the word when the ridges are obscured. There is no way to put an automatic station on every hill and in every river bottom area, though, so pilots will forever be left to interpret and interpolate. The hazard comes when a pilot sets out with a determination that the weather is going to be okay—wearing rose-colored glasses, if you will—and presses on with the thought that the reported weather behind is good, the reported weather to one side is good, the reported weather at a station up ahead is good, and the forecasts are good, so it's bound to be okay to fly on regardless of how bad it looks through the windshield. Visual is VFR's first name, so what the pilot sees just has to be assigned a lot of weight in the decision process.

Help from Below

Another contributing factor, a rather insidious one, is the feeling some pilots have that people on the ground can truly help an airplane in flight. This concept suggests that it might be okay to fly on until belly button deep in alligators and then call and transfer the mess to Big Brother. There are some situations in which a person on the ground can give meaningful help to a pilot in distress by giving location or soothing advice, but fate is squarely in the pilot's hand a great majority of the time.

It is interesting to contemplate that back in the good old days before radio, pilots made a lot of precautionary cow-pasture landings in bad weather. This was that day's form of going for help after pressing on too far, and it worked rather well. Now the airplanes don't do so well in pastures, so perhaps the feeling has changed to one of calling for help, calling the FAA as an "out," except that this modern version of going for help often doesn't work. The pilots of the good old days could, for a fact, extricate themselves with the precautionary landing because in so doing they satisfied the basic responsibility of flying the airplane until it stopped. Picking up a microphone does not satisfy that basic responsibility.

Blue Shield

Another factor contributing to modern-day complacency is the smattering of instrument training given to student pilots. This could lead a person to believe that "I can handle it" after flying inadvertently into cloud. Some perhaps can, especially if they work at maintaining proficiency, but many private pilots lose instrument proficiency and find themselves unable to fly instruments when the chips are down. Another fact argues strongly against the value of limited instrument training. Every year there are a substantial number of "continued VFR" accidents in which the pilot actually has an instrument rating. How can you explain an instrument pilot breaking an airplane trying to fly VFR in marginal weather? For one thing, the hardness of rock is unimpressed by FAA ratings. Also, there are instances of loss of control—inability to fly on the gauges—by instrument pilots. Perhaps they just can't perform when suddenly thrust into IFR conditions. The key to VFR is staying VFR regardless of the words on your license.

One of the prime things we learn when combining and considering the factors in the first stage of a VFR weather-related accident is that the pilot must learn to isolate flying from other things and fly only on the basis of aeronautical right and wrong. If the flight is continued on the basis of business or pleasure, if clouds are viewed through rose-colored glasses, and/or if the pilot flies into a mess feeling secure because of available help from the ground or minimum instrument instruction in basic flight training, then conditions are set for the second stage.

Second Stage

Discussion of the first stage is related to thought processes. There's some of that in the second stage, too, but there are also statistics to use in drawing a picture of what happens in VFR weather-related accidents. For example, we know that the bulk of the accidents occur en route, when pilots either fly into the ground still in control of the aircraft or when they hit the ground riding as a passenger, having lost control of the aircraft. The latter accounts for a slightly higher percentage of the accidents, but let's look first at the pilot who continues VFR into adverse weather and then flies into the ground, in control of the airplane.

Mountains

This type of accident happens in several ways. One way, a very popular one, is to just fly into high terrain. Perhaps you recall the Texas International Airlines Convair 600 crash of a few years back. It was a classic case of continuing VFR into adverse weather conditions and then flying into high terrain. The pilots were unsure of their exact position, and the cockpit voice recorder overheard one pilot saying that the highest terrain in the area where they were flying was 1,200 feet. Not long afterward, the crew flew the airplane into a 2,600-foot hill at about the 2,000-foot level. They learned the hard way that mountains are where you find them, not where you think they are. Many general aviation airplanes are lost in this manner every year, and special problems arise when pilots accustomed to flying in flat country tackle the mountains in adverse weather conditions. In fact, almost half the general aviation airplanes that become the subject of search-and-rescue missions are lost in mountainous terrain in marginal VFR conditions.

Flat Country

Not all hit mountains, and a VFR pilot running the scud in flat country can fall victim to an erroneous old superstition that there's always a ceiling: Fly low enough and you can see. More than one pilot has entered IFR conditions and then started a descent to get below the clouds only to find the ceiling about halfway down the old oak tree. Another way people frequently fail is in trying to turn around in scud and cloud after things go sour on a railroad- or highway-following flight plan. Roads, rail and otherwise, often follow the lowest ground, so any turn might be toward higher ground. Also, if the airplane is only a couple of hundred feet off the deck, that much altitude is easy to lose in a turn. Losing 200 feet in a turn doesn't qualify as loss of control, but it can be disastrous in certain situations.

However it is done, most of the pilots who fly into the ground in adverse weather do a complete job of wrapping things up. The airplane is almost always moving along at normal cruise, which is usually too fast for survival. There are exceptions, but the exceptions usually come when the airplane is being operated at speeds lower than normal cruise. One I know of involved flight into a hillside during a climb. The pilot just hit the hill without seeing it, but speed was low and the angle of impact was moderated by the airplane's climb angle. The occupants were hardly scratched. Shoulder-harness systems help a great deal in such situations.

Loss of Control

When a VFR pilot enters adverse weather conditions and then loses control, one of two things happens: The airplane hangs together until it hits the ground or the airframe fails in flight. These two areas need to be statistically separated for basic discussion.

In the great majority of accidents, the airplane reaches the ground in one piece after the pilot loses control. In about 20 percent of the accidents, the pilot overstresses the airplane and at least some part of it fails before the airplane hits the ground. In either case, the cause is the same: The pilot lost control. The technical difference in outcome really has little bearing on the accident and is related more to the configuration of the aircraft than anything else. When a pilot loses control of an aerodynamically clean airplane, which certainly means it has retractable gear, the airspeed tends to build very rapidly unless the pilot extends the gear and closes the throttle. The airspeed moves into the yellow caution area and soon flirts with the red line. The airplane usually establishes itself in a spiral dive—a stable maneuver with high airspeed, steep angle of bank, and a steep nose-down attitude. The airplane probably doesn't break itself in the spiral dive, but at high airspeed it doesn't take much additional g-load to put tons more load on the structure than it was designed to stand. Breakup comes in a recovery attempt: Level the wings and pull out of the screaming dive. Or perhaps the pilot senses the "dive" more strongly than the "turn" and pulls the airplane apart in the spiral.

The theory has been advanced that the lighter the longitudinal control forces, the higher the incidence of airframe failure in flight. That theory might have some basis—statistics could be developed that would tend to bear it out—but the final outcome of the event might not be so different. Once a VFR pilot loses control on instruments, only a stroke of luck is likely to salvage the flight. And if you take the total of loss-of-control accidents, the various makes and models tend to come out about even. Some just specialize in breaking before they hit the ground rather than after. This will be covered fully in chapter 8.

Thunderstorms

Thunderstorms play a role in about half the VFR weather-related airframe failures in flight. There actually tend to be more airframe failures in thunderstorm areas involving VFR than IFR flights. This is still more of an IFR subject, so it will be treated fully in chapter 2. The VFR pilot who continues and winds up in cloud is in a perilous state; make that cloud a cumulonimbus and there is not much left to discuss.

Preliminaries

Regardless of what happens after a loss of control, the preliminaries probably have something in common. Disaster strikes when the pilot is diverted from the basic task of keeping the wings level. This might happen almost instantly, as when entering the turbulent clouds of a thunderstorm, or it might take a while. At times, a noninstrument pilot gets off to a good start and manages for a considerable time on instruments, only to lose control because of a diversion. Perhaps a little turbulence is the straw, or it could be something simple like time taken to look at a map or fool with a radio. The sum of the accidents strongly suggests that a VFR pilot trying to fly gauges should concentrate on the basics for a while before doing anything else and should never stray very far from the basics. There might be a great compulsion to look at a chart, turn right, turn left, go up, go down, or use the radio, but in the final analysis the pilot is probably going to save himself with the ability to keep the airplane right side up. Settling in with that for a moment before fooling with anything else would have to be considered best in most situations.

Whereas the pilot who flies into the ground under control usually does so suddenly—soon after entering inclement weather or reaching high terrain—the pilot who flies into cloud, does not hit something, and survives the first few minutes on instruments still has a chance. He gets to make a few more mistakes, or to make up for past mistakes, by doing it correctly. It is from these incidents that the dramatic tape recordings of pilot-controller conversations are developed—these are usually the unsuccessful events. There are occasional successful saves—perhaps enough to create the image that there is a life preserver hanging on the clouds—but the bad outcomes outnumber the good. Real success lies in staying out of the clouds when flying VFR.

Pilot Understanding of Risk

Weather-related accidents involving VFR pilots pose quite a dilemma. A person who learns to fly can only be expected to quickly develop the desire to put flying to practical use. The next step is to start pushing the horizons back. Then the time comes when there is adverse weather between the pilot and an intended destination, and the fine line between possible and impossible becomes the challenge and the problem.

To some, the problem is simple once the ingredients are

understood. The VFR pilot in adverse weather conditions is breaking the law, doing something he was not trained to do, and flying in a manner contrary to the advice of more knowledgeable pilots. The government might try to treat the problem by raising the VFR minimums, but that is a questionable way to do it. New rules would be just as easy to break as old ones. Also, VFR weather minimums are as diffuse as cloud. Who really knows when an airplane is 2,000 feet horizontally from a cloud? I've never seen a tape measure that long. More training is another cure that is often advanced, and this would help if the training addressed the proper area—the nitty-gritty of interpreting weather in person.

Human nature being what it is, the best remedy is in pilot understanding of the risks involved. A small percentage of the flying is done by VFR pilots in adverse weather conditions, but a very high percentage of the serious general aviation accidents involve VFR pilots in adverse weather conditions. A pilot flying VFR without three miles visibility and without a ceiling that is at least 1,000 feet above the highest obstacle five miles either side of the proposed flight path is simply engaging in one of the most hazardous forms of flying. No question about it, that's just not the way to fly weather.

2 | IFR Weather-Related Accidents

There is a substantial difference in the risk involved during marginal VFR flight and IFR flight. Whereas scud running is an inexact aeronautical science involving a continuous high level of risk, IFR might be classified as the most precise form of flying with higher risk limited to a small percentage of the time. There is a procedure and a number on the chart for virtually everything in IFR; the pilot's work is to match the numbers on the panel with the numbers on the chart.

The nature of the two forms of flying tells us that marginal VFR is by far the riskiest, but it is not possible to put an exact value on the IFR advantage over marginal VFR because no figures are available on the amount of hours flown in each category. We do know that 20 percent of the fatal weather-related accidents in general aviation involve instrument-rated pilots flying on IFR flight plans, and we can at least contemplate some conclusions from this figure. If marginal VFR hours and IFR hours are equal, then IFR is four times safer. It is likely that IFR hours flown exceed true marginal VFR hours, though, so it should be accurate to say that the VFR version of trying to get there when the weather is bad involves more than four times the risk of flying IFR. The figure might be twenty times if all the necessary ingredients were available for a true determination. So IFR capability offers far less risk and far greater utility —quite a combination. The IFR accident picture also suggests that the instrument-rated pilot can easily develop a guard against the most frequent accident causes.

Ice and thunderstorms are the two things that strike the most fear into the instrument-rated heart. There is ample opportunity for the IFR pilot to think about both, too, because depending on the time of year and the synoptic situation, one or the other is forecast as a possibility for a relatively high percentage of IFR flights. Much of this is a result of a forecaster covering every possible eventuality by forecasting the chance of something if there is the slightest possibility that it might exist. Don't dismiss it with that thought, though. When a forecaster offers the opinion that bad things are possible, it is done to forewarn the pilot.

The Chill Factor

Taking ice first, we find that general aviation pilots show a healthy respect for the frosty stuff because it was a factor in only six IFR accidents in a one-year period selected as an example. And it is heartening that you can study the circumstances in most ice-related accidents and imagine how the flight could have been flown to a successful, if not a routine, conclusion.

If a pilot has recurring nightmares about icing encounters, he's likely to dream the textbook horror story of tremendous ice accumulation in a few minutes. The airplane will become festooned with giant icicles and will finally crash to the ground because of the weight and deformity of the frozen decoration. A pretty good dream, but it seldom works that way. In the majority of ice-related accidents, the pilot stacks some other basic errors on top of the ice to create the impossible situation. This makes it important to look beyond the ice instead of shrugging and just saying that the ice did it.

One pilot crashed on approach in a well-iced airplane. It was the third approach to that airport, so the pilot must have wanted badly to land there. He persisted in the effort to land despite the ice, and it is entirely possible that the pilot would have descended into the ground without any ice on the airplane. In other words, the ice might have been incidental. This theme recurs in so-called icing accidents. As in this example, many low-level icing situations also involve low ceilings and fog, which in turn lead a pilot to take risks that might be unrelated to icing. The airplane crashes with ice adhering to it so that is listed as a factor. Perhaps it should just be listed as the last straw.

War Stories

It is interesting that even pilots with considerable IFR experience have relatively few really bad ice tales to tell. Perhaps this is because ice does develop slowly, giving time to
plan. Most pilots start planning quickly and develop an
alternate course of action that deals with the ice situation.
Even in serious icing situations, fast action is usually rewarding so war stories are minimized.

I have only one good ice tale—of a flight in a 250
Comanche. It was late December. The forecast had initially
been for clear weather over the entire New York-to-Dallas
route, but things were destined to become interesting. It
was raining when we stopped in Nashville, and a careful
rethink was in order.

Despite the fact the weather was worse than forecast, the
briefer saw no problem in an IFR flight to the Southwest.
Six thousand would be a good ice-free level, he said, so we
launched with that altitude requested.

The weather decided to do its icy thing before we
reached Memphis. The air became quite turbulent, and ice
started building rapidly on the Comanche. The surface
weather was having its problems, too, with ceilings and vis-
ibilities quite low in what was turning into a real snow-
storm. The time had come for a fast decision, and there was
no question in this case that the thing to do was land as
soon as possible. There were a couple of small airports
available with instrument approaches, but I chose Memphis
because of its full instrument landing system. A missed
approach would be a bad deal, and I was motivated to fly
that ILS with some precision. It all worked well, but the

airplane wouldn't have been good for many more miles had the ice continued to accumulate.

The elapsed time from the first collection of ice to landing was probably not over thirty minutes. The moral was that ice is bad, but it can be handled if something is done about it. That "something" would almost never be a continuation of the present status.

Watch the Basics

Once ice appears and something is done to get away from it the record is clear in suggesting that the pilot pay careful attention to the aerodynamics of ice as well as to minimum altitudes and other staples. Many ice-related accidents end in a stall and spin, which comes about after the pilot has mastered everything but the final approach and landing. In one such event, the pilot collected a respectable but not debilitating amount of ice and then stalled while turning on final approach after making an instrument approach. The surface wind was strong and across the runway, and in setting up the circle for landing after breaking out of the clouds, the pilot had elected to circle to the left. By so doing, he subjected the airplane to a very strong downwind component on base leg. The additional ground speed caused an overshoot of the turn onto final; the pilot probably steepened the bank to try to complete the turn, and zap, the airplane stalled and started to spin. The ice on the wings no doubt contributed to the accident, but it was far from the sole cause. The outcome might have been the same without the ice.

The weight and deformity of ice does increase the stalling speed of an airplane. Another thing it can do is foul up the airflow over the tail of an airplane when the flaps are extended. As a result, the use of flaps is not recommended when flying with ice on many or most airplanes. The pilot's operating handbook should have the word on this. Ice plus no flaps would call for careful calculation of proper approach speed. Some knots would need to be added for ice in addition to the extra speed required for a no-flap approach.

Twins in Ice

In the full year's accidents used as an example, it is interesting to note that all six airplanes in ice-related accidents were twins. Some carried deicing equipment. Why might this be? I suspect that pilots flying singles are more attuned to the theory of alternative action in case of trouble and thus do a more prompt job of fleeing ice at the first sign of it. Twin-engine pilots might be taken by the "big iron" syndrome: "I can fly through hell for love in my airplane because it has two engines." The risk involved in ice is hardly altered by the number of engines on an airplane. And even though a twin probably has better climb capability than a single going into an icing situation, the twin probably loses that capability quicker because it offers greater surface area for ice collection than does a single of comparable airframe size. Two-engine nacelles and a big bare nose can collect a lot of extra ice in a hurry.

Geography

The geography of icing accidents is also interesting. The worst dream about ice calls for the airplane to be unable to maintain altitude in mountainous terrain, and while this does happen, four of the six icing accidents in our sample year happened in flat country. Perhaps this is an illustration that pilot fear of ice is multiplied in rough terrain, especially in the Rockies, and people are more careful about staying away from the stuff there.

Positional awareness and a knowledge of the terrain are important ice-related items when flying in rough terrain. Knowledge of the ridge locations (and height) and the valley locations in relation to the position of the airplane can save the day. The snap judgment might be that the closest airport is the best one to head for, but if it is dark, there's no weather reporting at that airport and only a VOR approach, and there are ridges in the area, an ILS airport in a wide valley a few miles farther away might be by far the best deal.

The relatively small number of ice-related IFR accidents, and the fact that ice is not the sole cause in most instances, should not belittle the importance of the risk that comes with icing encounters. The risk is there, and it probably

increases as the square of the time spent flying in icing
conditions. The only answer to ice is to get out of it: Climb,
descend, retreat, or land.

Thunder

Thunderstorms appear in the IFR accident column with
about the same frequency as ice; there were seven in the
sample year. The similarity ends there. Thunderstorms are
an either/or situation: Either you are in one or you are not.
Whereas a pilot's ice planning might reach a peak after ice
has started to accumulate, a pilot's thunderstorm planning
had best start before the airplane is in one of the beasts.
There is a contrast in equipment involved in thunderstorm
accidents in our sample year, too. Only two of the seven
thunderstorm aircraft were twins. Perhaps singles fly more
IFR hours than twins and thus have greater exposure, but
there should be more to it than that. It is an interesting
place to start examining the thunderstorm question.

One prone to jump to conclusions might say that twins
have less thunderstorm accidents because they are bigger
and stronger. There could be some logic to that, but the
thought is still misleading. The strength requirement for
general aviation airplanes is built around two factors,
g-loading and the consideration of a vertical gust of a given
strength. The requirements are identical for all airplanes
weighing under 6,000 pounds. Above 6,000 pounds, the
g-loading requirement decreases, but the vertical gust that

must be considered remains the same. This leaves the impression that all airplanes are equal in thunderstorm turbulence, regardless of size, wing loading, and speed. This is also misleading for several reasons.

There Is a Difference

First and foremost, anyone who has ridden through a thunderstorm in a large airplane and in a small airplane knows that there is a difference. The difference is not related to brute strength—the certification rules handle that—it is more often related to controllability. When airframe failure in flight occurs in a thunderstorm-related accident, it is usually established that the failure occurred after the pilot lost control of the airplane, not as the airplane initially entered an area of turbulence. (This, incidentally, is relatively easy to establish by studying the nature and sequence of the airframe failure.)

What loss of control tells us is that while large and small airplanes might be more or less equal in ability to withstand turbulence, they are apparently far apart in their ability to be flown in turbulence. Or, the pilots who fly them are not equal in ability. There is probably substance to both thoughts.

A lighter airplane is likely to be slower and will thus spend more time in turbulence. The possibility of losing control would have to be in direct proportion to the time spent in turbulence. Displacements will also be greater than might be the case with larger, faster, or heavier aircraft. Pit a forty-foot-per-second gust against an airplane flying at 100 knots and against an airplane flying at 200 knots, and while the g-load might be the same, the upward displacement of the faster airplane would be much less—just as a 40-knot crosswind would have less effect on the ground track of the faster airplane. Consider it in another light. The angle-of-attack increases in response to the gust in the 100-knot airplane would be half as rapid and the airplane's response to the change would thus take twice as long. Faster airplanes might develop relatively high g-loads while flying through the same bit of turbulence as a light airplane, but the ride in the faster or heavier airplane is felt more as sharp jabs, annoyances that come and go rather quickly, whereas the slower airplane wallows and pitches much more.

When considering the controllability of larger versus smaller airplanes, we must also acknowledge that the smaller airplane is more affected simply because of size. As it flies slowly through shear, eddies, and gusts, a greater percentage of the whole machine can be in the influence of the small but violent disturbances at one time.

Twins have another advantage over singles. Airborne weather radar can be fitted, and that is without a doubt a fine weather avoidance tool.

Experience

People who fly a lot in thunderstorm country find that the beasts always tend to be different and that avoidance is the only real key to success. You might note a pilot flying through an impossible-looking area without having a problem, and as you take a bite yourself there are times when the ferocity of a storm seems perhaps not so overwhelming. Then a bad experience changes all that.

I have a vivid recollection of one encounter. It was between Fort Smith and Little Rock, Arkansas. There was no radar in the airplane, and this was before the time of air route traffic control radar to help with weather avoidance. The briefing had suggested scattered thunderstorms, and the dark mass of sky ahead should have told me that they were scattered generously along my path. But that was no deterrent as I kept the nose of the rugged old Twin Bonanza pointed straight ahead.

The first sensation was of acceleration and g-load. The airspeed was increasing and the airplane was ascending; both were happening quite rapidly. Within the ascending air were staccato-sharp jabs. I've forgotten the amount of ascent, but it came to several thousand feet, even with the engines throttled back. I was concerned about not maintaining altitude but said nothing to the FAA controller (then CAA) about it. The microphone had fallen off its hook, and I felt that my time had best be devoted to taming the airplane. I also thought that any other airplane in there would also have been ascending.

I did consider turning around but hesitated because my ability was being sorely taxed by the straight-and-level

chore. I think it was a good decision, too, because in studying accident reports I have found quite a number in which
it appears almost certain that the pilot lost control as a
turn was attempted after a storm had been penetrated. The
best time to turn is before entering a storm. Also, it is often
noted that when an airplane crashes in a thunderstorm
area, the witnesses report that the heavy rain started after
the crash. This suggests that the worst turbulence might be
found around the edges of the heavy precipitation, not in it,
not once you have flown past the teeth of the storm and into
its gullet. Weather research tends to support this theory, so
presumably I did the right thing by continuing after making
the initial mistake.

Aerial Submarine

After the updraft came the heavy, the unbelievably heavy,
rain. It was like being in a submarine. The eroding effect of
the water took all the paint off the leading edges of the
almost new airplane. The turbulence remained in the rain,
but it did not seem as bad as before the water was reached.
The serious bumps did resume as I flew back out of the rain
area, and, in retrospect, the greatest difficulty in the turbulence came from not being able to see the instruments
clearly. The Twin Bonanza had a soft seat, and the panel
became a jumbled blur as I bounced up and down. The
airplane did have one of those big, old-fashioned, surplus
World War II artificial horizons; it was the easiest thing to
see so I finally just concentrated on it and nothing else.

Flying an approximate heading was not as much a problem as altitude control, but I could see where roll control would become quite a consideration in an airplane with less powerful lateral control than the Twin Bonanza.

So it can work. If avoidance fails, if the big mistake is made, it doesn't automatically mean total failure. The relatively low number of thunderstorm-related IFR accidents bears this out. Seven aircraft were lost in a year. How many do you suppose flew into what might be defined as a thunderstorm during that period? Seventy? Seven hundred? Seven thousand? Certainly it is safe to say that a lot more trespassed than were caught. This doesn't recommend the activity, but it does show that the error of entry is survivable, given a storm below the severe level and reasonable flying technique.

Hang in There

The airplanes are strong. All they ask is to be flown at a speed that will give the structure maximum protection. Maneuvering speed makes this offer to the pilot: If the indicated airspeed is at or below that value, there is no way for a storm to break the airplane. When the airplane is at maneuvering speed, a vertical gust will cause the airplane to relieve itself (by momentarily stalling) as the limit load factor is reached. At any speed above maneuvering, the airplane is vulnerable to an overstress situation. Below the speed, a vertical gust will make it stall at g-loads lower than the limit load factor.

It is best to anticipate turbulence. If maneuvering speed is below normal cruise, slow the airplane to maneuvering at the first hint that turbulence might lie ahead. It is better to fly a few extra miles at reduced speed than to impose unnecessary stresses on the old airframe. Once the bumps start, the pilot's job description calls for wings to be kept level, the pitch attitude to be kept as close to level as possible, and the airspeed to be maintained somewhere around maneuvering speed. In light piston airplanes with rapid power response, the elevator is used to control pitch attitude, and power should be used freely when the airspeed shows a marked move away from maneuvering speed.

It must also be noted that maneuvering speed decreases as weight decreases. If only one maneuvering speed is listed in the pilot's operating handbook, and that speed is for gross weight, the airplane should be flown somewhat slower than the listed speed when penetrating turbulence at a lighter weight. A rule of thumb is to reduce the maneuvering speed by half the percentage the airplane is below gross weight. For example, if flying a 2,300-pound aircraft at 2,070 pounds, 10 percent below gross, reduce the published maneuvering speed by 5 percent.

Controversy

The mention of maneuvering speed being lower at lighter weights always causes some controversy. This is fact, though, for a number of reasons. One is that lower weights often result from fuel burn, which means that the spanwise distribution of weight has changed, with more weight concentration toward the center of the airframe and higher bending loads on the wings in turbulence. Also, the lighter airplane will experience more rapid acceleration when entering a vertical gust of given strength. And while the reduced weight might mean reduced bending loads on the wings in cases where the spanwise distribution of weight has not changed much, the sharper accelerations cause more stress on other parts of the airframe. Pilots tend to think only of the wings in turbulent situations; in truth, the wings are often the last parts to fail when an airplane breaks up in flight. For instance, the horizontal tail or an engine mount might fail first.

A garden-variety thunderstorm is a rough, wild, uncomfortable, and high-risk place to be in a light (or heavy) airplane, but it is not a hopeless place. If the pilot understands the factors working for and against success and keeps his or her act together, the airplane is likely to respond in kind.

VFR v. IFR

One rather interesting statistic might go here as well as anywhere else. As mentioned in chapter 1, there are probably more airframe failures in thunderstorms involving VFR pilots than IFR pilots. The score in our sample year was 10 to 7, VFR over IFR. So, when you read of a thunderstorm accident, don't automatically consign it to an IFR pilot who flew into one and couldn't handle the situation.

You *can* almost consign each IFR thunderstorm accident to a pilot's failure to make every effort to stay out of storms. They just don't reach out, grab airplanes, and dash them to the ground. In a few cases, the pilot was receiving radar vectors from air traffic control radar, and on the surface this is perhaps a suggestion that the pilot was "trapped" even though he was using all available tools to avoid thunderstorm activity. Often, though, study shows that the pilot was trying to use radar advisories to penetrate areas of severe weather. This won't work every time with airborne weather radar, much less with traffic control radar. The rule is to stay twenty miles away from severe weather, regardless of radar availability. It must also be noted that the en route traffic control radar systems completed a change from broad-band radar to narrow-band computerized radar display in 1975. The argument over which radar system is best for weather display will probably never end, but the people who seem to know, the controllers and the pilots, tend to agree that the new weather radar systems are not as useful as the old for weather avoidance assistance.

Airborne Weather Radar

When considering the use of airborne weather radar, its value is underscored by the fact that an airplane with this equipment is seldom lost in a thunderstorm area. When a

pilot flying a radar-equipped airplane does lose an argument with a thunderstorm, it is usually the result of a pilot
using radar as a penetration rather than as an avoidance
tool. That is not what radar (or the airplane) was designed
for, and the guideline of staying twenty miles away from
severe storms (meaning all storms when severe weather is
forecast) and five miles away from other storms is true with
or without radar.

Pilots of most single-engine airplanes can't buy radar yet,
which leaves weather avoidance primarily to the eyeball,
with some help from traffic control radar. This means that
some flights will have to be canceled unless the pilot is
willing to accept an increase in risk, along with a possible
thorough trouncing.

The Biggest Problem

Thunderstorms, like ice, command respect. Their menace is
apparent, and warnings about staying away from them are
plentiful. They rank high on the least-wanted list: Ask IFR
pilots what bugs them most and it'll be thunder or ice, depending on the region of the country. In truth, though,
these two things are only the tip of the iceberg. There is a
silent and invisible IFR problem that accounts for more
than 50 percent of the total IFR accidents—over twice as
many as ice and thunderstorms combined. One reason it
retains mastery over pilots is because it is not obvious. The
severity of it can't be seen growing on the wing or flashing

in the sky, and it can't be felt tossing the airplane about.
For a fact, the instrument approach is the site of most IFR
accidents, yet there are few pilots who are nearly as concerned about a low approach as they might be about a
cumulonimbus ahead or a growing white line of ice on the
leading edge.

Numero Uno

Virtually all instrument-approach accidents have something
in common. For one reason or another, a pilot leaves the
haven of a minimum safe altitude shown on a chart and
then flies the brightly painted collection of aluminum into
the earth. The reason is seldom related to the elements or to
the machine. Instead, the approach accidents can almost all
be charged either to poor procedures or to overzealousness.

Poor procedures? Certainly anything a pilot does that
results in an accident is a poor procedure. But in IFR we
find a special breed of procedural mistakes that is related to
misreading or misunderstanding a chart. Some examples
include an incorrect direction or turn on a missed approach, an attempted circling approach below circling minimums, or a descent to an altitude lower than the safe
minimum on the chart. In the latter case, the reference is
not to the final approach segment. When pilots descend
below the minimum on final, I think it is almost always
chargeable to overambition in wanting to find the ground
and land, or to a reliance on visual flying when the actual
clues are inadequate or misleading.

The chart-reading mistakes are in a minority on IFR approach accidents, even though one of the most publicized airline accidents of all time, the 1974 Thanksgiving weekend TWA crash near Dulles, was related to this problem. Still, reading a figure incorrectly can lead to serious consequences and is something to guard against.

Accidentally on Purpose

The nature of most IFR approach accidents strongly suggests that the descent was intentional. In some instances the pilot might break the rules by leaving the minimum descent altitude (or decision height if on an ILS) before sighting the runway, the approach lights, or other markings identifiable with the approach end of the runway. This takes a lack of imagination, because minimums provide truly minimum clearances over the ground and over obstacles. In most cases, the minimum altitudes flown during an IFR approach are actually much lower than a pilot would find comfortable, or would normally fly, in VFR weather. If a pilot tempted with "busting" minimums would take a moment to visualize the rocks and trees reaching hungrily for the belly of the airplane, such temptation might fade.

There are a few other IFR considerations. Those that relate to mechanical factors are covered in chapter 8, on the relative problems of singles and twins. Occasionally we see a case of an instrument-rated pilot on an IFR flight plan losing control of the aircraft in normal conditions. This, though, isn't very common and can almost always be charged to a pilot moving in over his or her head. Either the pilot is rusty or allows some distraction to divert attention from the primary duty of keeping the airplane upright.

The concentration of IFR accidents in one phase of flight, the approach, suggests that IFR risk management shouldn't be complicated. Methodical self-discipline should handle the temptations that lead to approach accidents. The other two biggies, ice and thunderstorms, are probably best avoided simply by not kidding yourself about what is flyable and what isn't. Also, as we will see in the next chapter, the condition of light has a very marked effect on the IFR accident record. This, too, should give us knowledge to use in minimizing risks while flying IFR.

3 | Night Flying

Night flying is one of the more utilitarian uses of the general aviation airplane, but many feel there is extra risk connected with flying around in the dark.

On the plus side, you can finish a day's work, fly into the night, and be at home or wherever else you might want to be the next morning. In many instances, a few hours of night flying can effectively save almost a whole day. Night flying can also cut travel costs by eliminating extra evenings with the innkeeper.

But isn't night flying foolhardy, especially in single-engine airplanes? If the engine quits, zap, you are zapped. Many a pilot has contemplated that unhappy event while gazing down into inky space and has forever sworn off the use of single-engine airplanes at night for fear of engine failure. That is an understandable human emotion, but it is without basis in fact. The things that hurt in the dark are seldom related to actual mechanical failure, and I've always wondered if perhaps the bad, the really bad accident rate at night might not have some relationship to pilot fear of engine failure in singles. There might be a widespread feeling that the engine is the only key to longevity when flying in the dark. There is nothing else to worry about as long as the engine runs. The record shows that such a feeling couldn't be further from the truth.

The VFR Picture

The great majority of serious night accidents are related to weather, not to mechanical considerations. In one year's time, a full 60 percent of the fatal night accidents involving VFR flights were weather-related. Looking at both day and night fatal weather accidents involving attempted VFR flights, we see that of the total, over 30 percent of this type of mishap happens in the dark. What percentage of the VFR flying is at night? In studying available figures on the number of flight plans filed at night and in using an FAA survey on air traffic activity, one can become convinced that somewhat less than 10 percent of the general aviation flight hours are in darkness.

At least 30 percent of the accidents in less than 10 percent of the time bears quite a message, and however you interpret those figures, they isolate night VFR as an extremely risky way to go cross-country when the weather isn't good. In fact, a case can be made for flying VFR cross-country at night only when the skies are clear or near-clear.

Double Obscurement

A lot of factors influence the risk involved in night VFR. The most important one is the simple fact that you can't see in the dark. This reduces night flying to instrument flying except on a clear night with a substantial moon and when flying over large, lighted metropolitan areas in good weather. Even if a pilot thinks he is flying VFR and is licensed only for VFR, survival depends on information from the instrument panel when it is really dark out. Avoiding terrain is a function of knowing the elevation and flying at a safe altitude, as indicated on the altimeter. Where a pilot might successfully hedgehop in the daytime by eyeball, seldom referring to the altimeter, the situation reverses at night. Then the altimeter and knowledge of position are prime considerations. The altimeter works as well at night, but consider the relative difficulty of keeping up with position at night. Pilotage navigation is highly approximate, and radio navigation is often of limited usefulness if flying low. Also, radio navigation would carry with it the requirement to correlate the position suggested by the equipment with the terrain.

Next Key

Missing the terrain is only part of the night VFR problem, too. Another key to success is in staying out of cloud. Clouds, unfortunately, are not marked, and a VFR pilot can inadvertently fly into cloud at night quite easily. The stage is then set for spatial disorientation and loss of control. Rain areas are also difficult to see in the dark.

Pilot Experience

The experience level of pilots who unsuccessfully tangle with inclement weather at night adds an interesting piece to the puzzle. Half are pilots with less than 300 total flying hours, and quite a few are student pilots. That is a low experience level to pit against a cloudy night, and it seems almost possible to write this group off with one thought: They simply did not understand the difficulty of the task and the high risk involved.

In most cases nothing helped them understand because no night flying experience was required of private pilots for years. Then the rules were changed to require either three hours of night flying for private pilot applicants or a daytime-only license. A special requirement for at least ten night landings suggests that the Feds think landing the airplane is the toughest part of doing it in the dark. That's part of it, true, but landing at night is certainly less difficult than flying night VFR cross-country in marginal conditions.

The night and day legal VFR minimums are the same, too. This is an additional suggestion to a new pilot that there is no substantial difference between daylight and dark. Combine the lack of emphasis in training with the lack of regulatory guidance, and then the unfortunate night record and the involvement of relatively inexperienced pilots becomes more understandable. The minimum amount of instrument training required of new private pilots could also bear on this by making a pilot look on loss of visual reference as a somewhat less than critical matter.

Purpose

Almost three-fourths of the ill-fated night flights were for pleasure or personal transportation. This use accounts for 35 percent of the total general aviation cross-country flying. Three-fourths of the accidents on one-third of the flights suggests that there must be a strong connection between the two things. One might ask what the purpose of the night flight should have been to make it safer. Why do we fly better at night when on business than when flying for personal reasons? Perhaps it is because the pleasure user is trying to add something to his activity by flying at night, and the pressure to complete it without interfering with a primary activity is great. The business user flying at night is doing something that is related to a primary activity. Also, pleasure use might involve playfulness on local flights, and an airplane isn't a very safe nighttime toy.

It is noteworthy that in one year there were no night weather-related accidents in instructional flying. That perfect record might be an indication of an almost total lack of activity, a lack that sends new private pilots flying away on dark nights with little or no training.

Single-Engine

The single-engine airplane is predominant in night accidents. Almost 95 percent of the airplanes that crash at night are singles. About 85 percent of the total airplanes are singles, so there is some truth to the fact that singles are relatively more lethal than twins at night. This becomes even more true when you consider that twins probably average more night use than singles. But the problem is not related to the number of engines; it is related to the risks taken by pilots in relation to weather.

The singles in night weather accidents involving VFR flights are generally traveling-type airplanes: four-place with a generous number of retractables included. The load factor is high in night weather-related accidents, with an average of 2.35 people on board each airplane. (The average for single-engine airplanes in all cross-country operations is 2.1.)

Holidays and Weekends

Many weather-related night accidents are associated with weekends or holiday periods. That is a natural connection. Leave after work on Friday and return after playing all day on Sunday. Or do the same thing around a holiday. Put it all together—night, some passengers, the need to get back to work, and then throw in some weather along the way. The pressure on the pilot increases with each ingredient.

If you have a business appointment with John Smith at Monday noon and the morning dawns cloudy and cruddy, it isn't so difficult or awkward to call Smith and tell him the sad tale. But if you find yourself 300 cloudy and rainy miles from home and work at seven o'clock on Sunday evening and John Smith is your boss, the conversation with him might be more strained. All these factors clearly define a primary area for risk management.

Night IFR

Whereas the weather-related night situation involving VFR flights is logical and relatively easy to rationalize, the IFR situation poses more questions. In the accident totals without regard to condition of light, we see IFR as a relatively low-risk, methodical operation. But when night is separated from day, the general aviation IFR pilot shows a clear weakness. The concept of matching numbers on the panel with numbers in the chart for good results crumbles in the dark. From 10 to 15 percent of the IFR flights are flown at night, and fully 50 percent of the general aviation IFR accidents occurred at night during a one-year period.

The night IFR pilots who have problems bear no resemblance to their relatively inexperienced VFR counterparts. In one year, pilots with over 10,000 total flying hours accounted for almost 20 percent of the night IFR accidents and outnumbered under-1,000-hour pilots by about two to one on the accident roster. Virtually all pilots involved in night IFR accidents held either commercial or airline transport pilot certificates, with the latter august group accounting for 30 percent of the problems. Three-fourths of the airplanes were twins.

Quick Explanation?

One explanation for the unhappy night IFR record quickly comes to mind: All those tired old airplanes flying cargo and mail around in the dark must be the root cause of the problem. Not so. In fact, while they do account for a substantial percentage of the night IFR operations, cargo air taxi operations were involved in less than one-fourth of the night fatal IFR accidents. And if you especially worry about the old twin Beech fleet that carries most of the mail, don't. Only one cargo-carrying twin Beech was involved in a fatal IFR accident during the one-year period studied. That particular accident had nothing to do with the airplane: The pilot flew the old bird into the ground short of the runway on a foggy night.

We noted that a high percentage of the pilots involved in accidents while flying VFR into adverse weather at night were on pleasure or personal transportation missions. There is no such corner on the night IFR accident market, where the uses are almost equally divided among personal transportation, business, corporate (meaning flights with a hired pilot), and air taxi cargo and passenger flights. This cross section eliminates any thought about a strong correlation between night IFR and type of use. Despite its regimentation and procedure, IFR is just one of those things that the general aviation pilot doesn't do as well in the dark.

The instrument approach is, as you might expect, the site of most night IFR accidents. The "premature arrival," as it is often called, reaches a peak after sunset. A contributing factor (but no excuse) is the lack of precision approach facilities with glide path guidance at general aviation airports. Also, many of the approaches call for circling. It has always seemed to me that a night circling approach in precipitation is the most exacting procedure in flying, and the record tends to support this theory. Perhaps the night IFR pilot really has the same trouble as the night VFR pilot because the last portion of the approach, after breaking out of the clouds, is really a rather difficult version of marginal VFR.

Illusions

Visual cues at night are purely lousy, and if one key factor could be assigned to night IFR approach difficulties it would probably have to be pilot reliance on erroneous visual cues. At the trying time after transitioning from instruments to visual flying, the only lights that can really help a pilot judge the descent are the lights on the runway of intended landing. Even the full approach lighting system on an ILS cannot help a pilot judge a descent angle. Why? It is a matter of the aiming point supplying the only valid visual cue on a visual approach. And if the aiming point is not the end of the runway, then the pilot is about to make the National Transportation Safety Board's computer whirl for a millisecond to count off one more who disregarded that fact. A pilot who leaves the safety of a minimum descent height or decision height at night without the runway lights in sight is looking for trouble.

According to the good book, the approach lights or any other marking identifiable with the end of the runway are excuse enough to descend. But if you want to preserve the old tail, insist on the runway itself, because all that's legal isn't safe.

Illusions plus Temptations

The nature of lights can lead a pilot down a perilous path at night, too. For example, you might shoot an approach, still be in cloud, and yet catch glimpses of the lights as the runway is overflown. This suggests that another try might be in order, perhaps at a somewhat lower altitude. That is a risky temptation and one that might not appear in the daytime when nothing but a gray mass would be sliding beneath the airplane as it plunges merrily through the murk. Some say that night approaches are easier because lights tend to be more visible than, say, just a runway by day. They might be easier to see, but what you see can hurt instead of help unless the limitations of the visual cue are recognized.

I think it a good reminder for day or night IFR to occasionally shoot approaches in good weather with no hood on. The descent to the minimum altitude, and flight at that altitude in visual conditions, is always a good illustration of how close you are to the ground when level at the minimum descent altitude or decision height. Then when shooting an approach to Jackass Flat on some dark and rainy night you can think back to what it looked like in daytime visual conditions. That should be enough to discourage any thoughts of a premature descent.

Thunder and Lightning

The annual night IFR accident sample is small enough (about thirty) that some variations do occur. In one year I found almost no thunderstorm-related night accidents; in another year thunderstorms were factors in a substantial percentage of the night IFR accidents. The strongest thought here is that storms are equally mean day or night and that while you might think they would be easier to avoid at night (because lightning is visible), there is probably no appreciable difference in the avoidance chore that might be based on the condition of light. True, at night you can always fly with the lightning at your back and avoid storms. But it is equally true that you can always fly with the cauliflower-shaped or dark clouds at your back in the daytime and avoid thunderstorms. I doubt if many pilots have flown into a cumulonimbus day or night without at least some knowledge that one was around and some apprehension about the hue of the sky, be it illuminated by lightning at night, or dark and ominous by day.

Weather Summary

IFR or VFR, the record is clear in showing that the general aviation pilot manages risks poorly when combining weather and night flying.

There is no solution as such to the night VFR weather question, avoidance is the only key. The wise VFR pilot would limit night cross-country flights to much better than minimum VFR weather, preferably clear skies, and would rely on the altimeter and not the eyeball for terrain clearance. A guideline might be never to fly lower than 2,000 feet above the highest obstacle within ten miles of the proposed flight path. If that can't be done at night in good VFR conditions, then it's time to be on the ground.

The IFR pilot's primary goal should be awareness of visual limitations at night. Not leaving the minimum descent altitude or the decision height until the runway lights are in sight is a good guard against the most common night IFR problems.

The night IFR pilot should also realize that the activity is one that few pilots engage in very often. Thus there are not many people who are really proficient at night IFR. Total flying experience just doesn't count for much when you are groping around the airport in the dark trying to line up with a runway. This is the most difficult maneuver; it is probably also the least practiced one. Few pilots get hood practice at night, and I don't know that it would be a very good simulation anyway. The message is to recognize the risks in night IFR and avoid them in a methodical manner.

The Other Items

In discussing IFR and VFR weather-related problems, we've covered about two-thirds of the night fatal accidents. A substantial percentage of the remaining night fatals involve one of the easiest risks of all to manage, alcohol. There aren't as many drunk-pilot accidents as some sources would suggest, but there are still enough to recognize this as a problem. The drinking-pilot phenomenon will be discussed fully in chapter 12. More of these accidents happen at night simply because that is when many people do their drinking. Once the alcohol has been consumed and the airplane mounted, the condition of light doesn't have much to do with the outcome.

Fuel Exhaustion

Fuel exhaustion is another clearly identifiable cause of serious accidents at night. This is perplexing. If pilots are apprehensive about flying at night, logic would suggest very conservative fuel reserves for night flights. The record, though, shows that there might be relatively more fuel exhaustion accidents at night than in the daytime. Perhaps this is because fuel exhaustion would be much more likely to result in an accident in the dark.

Fuel exhaustion is a clear example of how the disciplines in flying work. About 200 general aviation pilots a year have an accident after running out of fuel. I can recall only one single case of an air carrier running out of fuel, a foreign carrier a number of years ago. Why do general aviation pilots run out of gas when airline pilots do not? Simple—airline pilots don't kid themselves about fuel, and they have the checks and balances of a dispatch system. There is a required reserve and this reserve is not violated. An air carrier might hold for improvement in weather, but when the moment comes that the holding is about to dip into the required reserve, it's off to the alternate, no question. In contrast, the general aviation pilot's only checks and balances are in thoughts of what it might be like to run out of fuel. Some pilots apparently lack imagination. And while most fuel exhaustion accidents involve singles, some involve twins. That would have to be one of life's dumbest feelings: Fly a twin because of a feeling that the engine-out capability might be useful and then use all the gas.

Why?

The reasons pilots run out of fuel at night are not valid, but they are factors and must be considered. To begin with, it is more difficult to buy fuel at night. Most airports close at sundown, so the night flyer must plan refueling stops carefully or wind up with a long way to go on a little fuel. Some fuel exhaustion accidents happen after relatively short flights that started with limited fuel on board, but most come after long flights.

Intentions are probably tolerable at the start of most fuel exhaustion flights. For example, the airplane holds four plus thirty worth of fuel; the time to the destination will be four hours, so that's thirty minutes extra. If there is a headwind, a stop can be made at Podunk just before dark to fly on with full tanks.

The real facts can become obscured as such a flight progresses, though. Perhaps the ground speed is three knots less than that used in calculating the thirty-minute reserve. Make the fuel stop based on that fact, or keep on flying and see? Maybe it gets dark a little earlier than anticipated and

Podunk doesn't answer the Unicom when called. Landing and finding no fuel might mean either delaying until the next morning or finding someone to come out and fill the tanks. Press on. The accident investigators often note that a pilot bypassed several lighted airports at night before using all the fuel and settling ignominiously into the darkness below. You do, however, have to recognize the fact that most of those airports were unattended at the time, and a landing would leave the airplane on a dark ramp with only the attention of the airport cat. The pilot knew that and it would have to be recognized as a factor. It is not a valid excuse for running out of fuel at night; it is just one of the reasons pilots do it.

Lost?

The relative difficulty of night navigation is another reason pilots run out of fuel at night. If a pilot flies with a thirty-minute reserve and then can't find the destination airport immediately, a very difficult situation arises.

One moral is that thirty minutes' fuel reserve is never enough. That is true day or night. We should really fly with a full and fat one-hour reserve calculated for every flight. That reserve should be considered an inviolate supply for emergency use only. No fair using even one pint of it to go on in the face of a slightly stronger-than-forecast headwind. Reserve fuel is for use when all else fails, for when the weather does an unforecast dirty trick, for when navigational ability fails you, or for when some mechanical problem introduces time-consuming procedure to the flight. The only proper pilot action when considering the use of reserve fuel for the normal part of a flight is to say: "This is stupid. We're going to make a fuel stop."

Fuel exhaustion is simply a product of the pilot's failure to think. Once I dug out a figure that is interesting to contemplate. In a large group of night accidents, the consequences of a forced landing at night after fuel exhaustion tended to be more serious than the consequences of forced landing after mechanical failure (which doesn't happen very often). Could it be that the pilot felt rather dumb after making the mistake of using all the fuel and could not perform in the forced landing?

Mismanagement

Another fuel problem is a factor in a substantial number of serious night accidents. Fuel might be on board, but the pilot mismanages it and winds up with the engine sucking on a dry tank or even on no tank. There are instances of a pilot actually turning the fuel off when intending to switch to the fullest tank or tanks before landing. This type of mistake tends to be serious when the pilot does it at an altitude too low to permit recognition and correction of the mistake. That bears a rather plain message: Take care of the tank switching at altitude.

The Nitty-Gritty

There are some night forced landings that are a product of mechanical failure, but they are few and far between. In fact, they account for a statistically insignificant part of the serious and total night accidents. For example, in 130 total night accidents (not a full year's supply), I found one engine failure on takeoff after which the pilot landed safely, one internal failure of an engine after which the pilot landed safely, one fire in an engine with a successful on-airport landing, one engine failure for unknown reasons after which the pilot ditched in a river and swam to shore, one failure for unknown reasons after which the pilot made a successful landing on a freeway, one on takeoff with an abort and a slide off the end, and one double-engine failure caused by Jet-A in 100-octane piston engines followed by a successful forced landing. There was no personal injury in these accidents. The airplanes suffered, of course, or they wouldn't have been classified as accidents. Just to give some comparison, in the same 130-night-accident sample there were 25 fuel-related accidents—either exhaustion, mismanagement, or water in the fuel (one)—and of the 25 fuel-related accidents, four were fatal.

Propellers

A rather unusual accident crops up often enough at night to warrant special note. Instances of passengers walking into propellers showed up three times in the 130-accident sample just noted. Needless to say, the results are always serious. It is difficult to imagine why this might happen more at night unless there is a tendency to let passengers get out while the engine is still running to go turn on car or hangar lights. Whatever, it is bad practice to let a passenger enter or leave an airplane with the engine running. An exception might be a twin, with the engine on the door side secured but the other one running. Even then, it would be unwise to let someone not familiar with flying machinery do much moving around the airplane when an engine is running.

Approach and Landing

Approach and landing accidents in good weather are quite common at night but are usually not serious. The majority happen during the landing itself, and there are some in which the pilot misjudges the approach and hits something short of the runway. While there's usually no personal injury connected with this type of accident, the potential for hurt is rather strong so it is worth more than a passing mention.

Take Careful Aim

The principles of flying to a runway are the same, day or night, fair weather or foul. It is a fact that the point on the ground toward which the airplane is flying remains stationary in the windshield as the airplane is flown at a constant attitude. Change attitude and the constant spot changes its position in the windshield. Change power or descend into a level with a different wind component, and things will change, but again one spot will appear to remain constant to the eye and the airplane will be tracking toward that spot. The runway lights make this rather easy to see at night.

The Slope

The protected slope for obstruction clearance on VFR approaches is supposed to be 20:1. That ratio applied to a ninety-knot ground speed means that a 456-foot-per-minute rate of descent will maintain standard obstacle clearance. Since all airports don't meet the protected slope, it would be good to add 50 percent to the minimum rate of descent and use a 700-fpm rate of descent on a ninety-knot approach to a VFR runway. The interaction between this and the constant spot theory is what keeps you out of the trees on dark nights. For example, if the spot remains constant with the airspeed on ninety knots, but the rate of descent is less than the acceptable amount (700 feet per minute), then the approach path is too shallow. Add some power and fly up to a steeper slope before resuming the descent.

(It's simple to determine the required rate of descent for a 20:1 slope. Convert speed to feet per minute and then divide by 20.)

IFR runways have a required 34:1 protected slope, so the situation is not as critical there, but it is good practice to always use a uniform approach slope at night for visual approaches. And the slope should be as steep as is safely practical in the type of aircraft flown.

What If?

One question always emerges toward the end of a discussion about the risks involved in night flying. Even though it is true that virtually all the engine failures at night are pilot induced, involving mismanagement of fuel or running out of gas, there is still some remote possibility that an essential engine part will give up the ghost and the cabin of a single-engine airplane will become quiet even though the pilot has done everything right. What then? It is easy to sit on the ground and pontificate over engines not quitting, but what do you do when one *does* fail at night?

There Is Hope

I suppose it is best to realize first that things are not hopeless. A very high percentage of the night forced landings are both survivable and survived. One key would be in touching down at minimum speed, but not stalling the airplane prematurely and reaching the ground in a spin or with a high sink rate. Another would be in not hitting some fixed object at a right or even a steep angle. Any stop will be very uncomfortable if it is sudden, but if the deceleration is spread over a period of time things won't be so bad.

I've heard it suggested that dark areas without lights might be cleared fields, good for night landings. They might be in Kansas, but in Arkansas such an area might more likely be forested or mountainous. At least it would be free of houses or power lines, though.

What if it is a mountain? Then it would be important to know the general ridge orientation in the area. You would certainly fare better coming down on a heading parallel to the ridges rather than doing it at right angles. This all suggests that pilot knowledge of the terrain is part of risk management at night.

In studying the charts to gain knowledge of the terrain, it is often possible to plan a route that will have inherent advantages. One night run I make frequently can be done one of two ways: Fly direct over some dark and rough terrain, or fly the north airway, only five miles longer, and stay within gliding distance of a river valley and four-lane highway all the way. It doesn't take much imagination to select the proper path.

Where To?

After a power failure the first impulse is to pick a place to go. Unless the goal is something that is easily identifiable, such as a four-lane highway, chances are that no really intelligent selection of landing area will be possible early in the glide from a normal cruising altitude at night. An exception would be with a moon or with an overcast and a lot of light reflection off the clouds over a populated area. Then something might be chosen early. In any case, turning the cockpit lights down to a very dim setting would help improve night vision. There are some things to do, too. Inform someone of the plight on the radio if possible, and try to get the engine going again. Switch mags, experiment with the mixture and the fuel selector, check the primer as locked, run the fuel pump, and do anything else that might change the status quo. Also, look for an airport. You'd sure hate to make a night forced landing in a random area if a lighted airport was within gliding distance.

How far can you glide? The glide ratio is in the pilot's operating handbook. It is a good thing to commit to memory.

At lower altitudes, landing lights can be a good aid in a night forced landing. How do you use them? The old joke is to turn them on and, if you don't like what you see, then turn them off. The value of the lights, though, is in giving the pilot last-minute choices. With lights plus the energy stored in a normal glide you can turn a little, flare, and keep flying to the last moment while remembering that the outcome will be successful if that sudden stop can be avoided. I would add that in such a situation a shoulder-harness system would be worth its weight in diamonds.

The End of a Perfect Day

Flying through the sunset and into the night is an experience that only pilots appreciate fully. It is interesting that the impact of the beauty of a day's retreat over the horizon is evident on the radio. The chatter almost always fades away as the sun sets. It is a reflective moment, during which a person is thankful for life and for the freedom of flight. After the beauty of the moment, though, carry on with the thought that it is a good thing to do only if the risks are recognized and managed, so that you may enjoy the sunrise, which is an equally beautiful time to reflect on the beauty of life and flight.

4 | Wind

Wind is natural to an airplane. After all, the only purpose of the propeller is to pull the machine forward and make wind over the wings. Wind can be weather, though, especially to the light airplane. It can have profound effects on the airplane as it moves up, down, and around. Just to play with words, it could even be said that wind is the number one hazard associated with thunderstorms. Those vertical currents that jab are, after all, only wind that is headed up or down. The same currents flow out of the storm, rearrange themselves parallel with the ground, and become the first gust and strong sustained wind found at the surface in a thunderstorm area.

Those winds are considered part of the thunderstorm subject. Just plain wind is also a factor in airplane accidents, and while the most frequent wind-related accident is found during landing, the breeze does its thing at other times. Strong winds across mountains can create turbulence. Strong headwinds can menace the fuel supply. Strong crosswinds can have a deleterious effect on takeoff and climb performance. Wind shear—changes in wind direction and velocity with altitude—can play strange and potentially lethal tricks.

How many accidents are attributable to wind? It is listed by name as a cause or factor in about 7 percent of the accidents. Wind, or the pilot's failure to understand wind, is probably a factor in more accidents than that, though. Some stall/spin accidents might be related to wind, and approach and landing accidents, in which a pilot misjudges distance and lands short, might be attributable to wind shear more often than the records indicate. It should also be noted that general aviation flying tends to diminish when the wind blows. Just compare the activity at the local airport on a very windy Sunday with the activity on a calm and beautiful Sunday. The bending rate per hour flown is undoubtedly much higher when the wind is blowing.

How Much Wind?

At what point does wind start becoming a real factor in general aviation operations? The answer to that question depends on several things. One is very simple: It is what you are accustomed to in the way of wind. In sections of the country where the wind often blows with vigor, pilots tend to continue routine operations in conditions that might not be considered acceptable in areas where strong wind isn't such a day-to-day event. One school I know of in windy country routinely allows solo student operations in Cessna 150s when the wind is as high as twenty-five knots. Dual flying is allowed in winds up to thirty-two knots. Some pilots might find those values uncomfortable, but if the airplane is properly handled they are really quite safe.

I've always wondered at what precise point we find true additional risk in high wind operations. When the wind is strong enough to rock the airplane around on the ground, it suggests that at some point the machine and the wind will do their thing. And you do occasionally hear of an airplane being blown over. But in exploring such incidents, there often seems to be a contributing factor, such as fast taxiing. The exact point at which you quit flying because of wind is thus a highly individual judgment. It is based on the airplane, the pilot, the airport, and, I suppose, also on the need to fly. The turbulence associated with high winds is often uncomfortable enough to answer the question for you and prompt the delay of a trip that isn't of great importance.

What Does It Do?

How does wind twist our tail when we bite off a bit too much of it? Starting at the beginning of a flight, there are some losses of directional control during crosswind takeoffs. Many thought that the advent of the tricycle-gear airplane would solve the directional control accident problem, but it did not. There's no magic to a tricycle; if you let the machine go its own way in a strong crosswind, it'll try the ditch every time.

The serious wind-related accidents in the departure phase usually come after takeoff, during the initial climb. Where there is trouble it often comes with a strong crosswind on an airport of marginal length for the operation. Obstructions upwind from the runway often add spice by making the gusty wind flow even more turbulent.

The problem here is caused by several things. For one, even if the crosswind is precisely steady in direction and velocity, the airplane's takeoff roll will be longer than in a calm wind condition. There is aerodynamic drag associated with the corrections necessary to offset the crosswind, and it is also an item of good practice to accelerate to a slightly higher-than-normal speed before lift-off in a crosswind.

Variable and Gusty

No strong crosswind provides an idyllic, steady, wind situation, and the variation in wind speed and direction might serve to prolong the takeoff even more. Any pilot who has flown much has experienced the crosswind situation in which the airspeed simply does not seem to increase for a moment during the takeoff run. In that situation, the wind direction has shifted more away from the nose of the airplane, or the velocity of a cross headwind has decreased. Things like this can happen at just the wrong time.

Once off the ground, the airplane is still subject to harassment by a strong crosswind. Wind just does not become steady and lose its gusty and shifty characteristics at a low altitude.

This is an appropriate place to address the subject of the wind's effect on an airplane in flight because wind can be used to advantage in the first stages of a climb, or it can be misunderstood to the point that the pilot's misuse of the airplane relative to the wind can result in an accident.

The Downwind Turn

The theory that the downwind turn is lethal has been the subject of much debate over the years. The argument is that once the airplane is free of the ground, a steady wind has no effect on airspeed whatsoever. Point it any way you wish, make 360s in strong winds; regardless of what you do the airspeed will not be affected by the wind. The ground track will be affected, to be sure, but the airspeed will remain constant. That is all very true. The other argument is that a low-altitude downwind turn will bite. That is also correct. For one thing, the low-level wind is seldom steady, and a gusty or variable wind does affect airspeed. For another, visual illusions lead a pilot to do the wrong things in a downwind turn.

This accident is a good illustration. It involved a go-around rather than a departure, but the principles are the same.

The crosswind was quite strong, and after aborting the landing attempt, the pilot elected to make a turn when a few hundred feet above the ground. The turn was in the normal traffic pattern direction, which just happened to be downwind. The airplane was not far into the turn when the angle of bank started increasing. Soon afterward, the airplane stalled and spun out of the bottom of the turn. The pilot was a victim of the downwind turn.

The Factors

Examine the things that happen in such a situation. First, turning downwind close to the ground has an immediate and dramatic visual effect. As the airplane turns, the groundspeed increases rapidly. Even if the wind is perfectly steady, and the airspeed and vertical speed are in fact unaffected, the increase in groundspeed will result in a much flatter climb gradient relative to the ground and any obstructions. The eye doesn't lie in telling the pilot about more forward speed and a flatter climb gradient relative to the ground. The eye does, however, make a very bad suggestion in such a case: It suggests that the nose of the aircraft should be pulled up to maintain the climb gradient. That is definitely not the right thing to do when airspeed might be critical.

Strong wind is never completely steady, and the nature

of wind relative to the ground couples with the illusion of a downwind turn to give a downwind turn just that much more lethal potential. Wind velocity tends to increase with altitude, so as the airplane climbs it is not operating in a steady wind. It might instead be flying with an increasing tailwind component, which causes some actual airspeed decay simply because the airplane does not adjust to the increase in wind instantly. Think of it like this: The airplane is flying at 90 knots indicated airspeed with a 10-knot crosswind. The groundspeed is about 90 knots. Turn downwind, climb, and suddenly increase that tailwind to 30 knots. What item is going to be most subject to immediate change? The airspeed. It won't drop an amount equal to the full increase in tailwind component, but it will drop some. The groundspeed of the airplane was at 100, and the airplane must accelerate to reflect the tailwind component and the 130-knot groundspeed that would result. Acceleration does not happen instantly, and the difference between the time it takes the tailwind component to increase 30 knots and the time it takes the airplane to accelerate 30 knots is some indication of the sag a pilot might see and feel when maneuvering into an increasing tailwind component. If the airplane is climbing, there might not be any more power to use in this acceleration. The only solution would be to lower the nose, further flattening the climb gradient. It takes discipline to do that, but it is important because if the airspeed is low to begin with, as in a climb, any airspeed decay moves the airplane into a higher drag condition nearer to the stall.

Question

Here we must digress for a moment to cover one question regarding the danger of a downwind turn. The increasing tailwind/decreasing airspeed business might lead you to believe that a steady wind does affect airspeed after all. When the airplane turns downwind in a steady wind, it is flying into an increasing tailwind, isn't it? Yes. But airspeed wouldn't be affected. The reason the airspeed is not affected turning downwind in a steady wind is because the airplane has already made its peace with the existing wind. The ground track was already affected by the crosswind (drift), and in a steady wind that effect simply translates to increased groundspeed as the airplane turns downwind—without bothering the airspeed. Wind affects airspeed only in gusty or gradient wind situations, when the actual direction or velocity of the wind changes abruptly.

Finally, as the airplane is banked for the downwind turn, one wing is actually at a higher altitude than the other and might be reaching up into a stronger wind. This would promote a strong overbanking tendency. Perhaps this seems farfetched in an airplane with a 35-foot wingspan, where the actual altitude difference of the wing tips in a thirty-degree bank would be only 17.5 feet. But the theory is valid, and there have been times when I think I've seen this effect in a downwind turn.

Upwind Turns

Most of the factors that work against the pilot in a down-wind turn work *for* the pilot in an upwind turn. Effective risk management in a strong crosswind situation thus suggests that any turns be made into the wind until at an altitude where the airspeed is at a very healthy value and climb capability is not critical.

En Route

What does wind do to you en route? The obvious things are related to groundspeed and comfort. The forecast winds aloft are often terribly inaccurate, and it is the pilot's responsibility to determine actual winds and not fly into a low-fuel situation because of a bad wind forecast.

Wind-induced turbulence can make the ride very uncomfortable—the stronger the wind, the worse the bumps, with the ante raised in direct proportion to the roughness of the terrain over which the wind is blowing.

As a strong wind blows over mountains, it can create turbulence so severe that it feels like the feathers are about to be plucked from the airplane's backside. Does such turbulence ever break an airplane? It can, to be sure, but it doesn't often do so. In one year there was but a single case of turbulence in clear air causing a serious general aviation accident.

Comfort is one reason we tend to stay out of real trouble

in clear air turbulence. It becomes extremely uncomfortable in the airplane long before any structural limit is reached, and as a result, the pilot is likely to slow the airplane down. Slowing down reduces the g-forces encountered at a given bump, and this serves the purpose of giving the structure even more margin, as well as contributing to occupant comfort. Maneuvering speed should be used whenever turbulence becomes uncomfortable.

Downdrafts

When flying in mountainous terrain, wind-induced turbulence might be the most obvious problem to the seat of the pants, but downdrafts on the lee side of the mountains can be an even greater hazard. It is not uncommon to see downdrafts that can exceed the rate of climb in general aviation airplanes, even over such relatively small mountains as the Appalachians. Both turbulence and downdraft considerations suggest that mountainous terrain be avoided when the forecast wind at ridge level is thirty knots or greater, unless the flight can be made at an altitude of at least 50 percent higher than the ridge levels. That does not guarantee a smooth ride, but it does help minimize risk.

The Arrival

Wind does its thing on departure and en route, but the arrival is where wind is likely to bring the most sweat to the palms of a pilot. The last phase of the flight is probably the most turbulent of all when surface winds are high, and if the pilot doesn't make a conscious effort to relax, the flying begins to resemble a wrestling match between airplane and pilot more than anything else. This serves to increase tension, and by the time the airplane is in the pattern, the stage might be set for error.

Wind effects in the traffic pattern have a definite bearing on a safe arrival when using a runway with a strong crosswind component. For example, consider a runway that runs to the north, runway 36, in a situation with a strong westerly wind—a rather common situation behind a cold front. If the pattern is left-hand, as most are, there will be a strong crosswind component from the right on downwind leg. The heading required will be 200 degrees if 20 degrees of drift is present. Then, on base leg, there will be a tailwind, if indeed a base leg is managed. Why trouble with base leg? For one thing, a turn of more than 180 degrees from the downwind leg heading will be required to bring an airplane around to a heading that will track the final approach course. If there's 20 degrees of drift on downwind, at least that much will be present on final, so the required turn from downwind to final will be 220 instead of 180 degrees.

Overshot Turn

A tailwind on base will also tend to make the pilot overshoot the turn on final. As that starts to unfold, the strong
tendency is to steepen the turn, hasten it on around. Perhaps a little bottom rudder might help. A bit more, and a
little steeper bank. Whoops, it spun. Do it every time in
such a situation.

Even though wind is not noted as a cause or factor in the
accident report, it is often possible to find very serious accidents that were prompted, promoted, or caused by a strong
downwind component on base leg. There are two ways to
manage this risk. Either fly a very wide pattern, and fly with
a firm resolve to go around if it appears that the turn onto
final isn't working well. Or go against the grain and fly the
pattern in the other direction, so that base leg will be into
the wind. The latter might be contrary to the regulation
requiring all turns to the left at uncontrolled airports unless
otherwise stipulated, but in extreme conditions such action
could be covered by the pilot's right to deviate from any
rule as required to meet an emergency. Avoiding a situation where a stall/spin might occur would seem to be
"meeting an emergency."

Approach Speed

Once the traffic pattern has been carefully planned, the
next thing is to select the final approach speed. The most

common error here is to use too much speed. As the airplane squirms, writhes, pitches, and rolls in low-level turbulence on a windy day, we all tend to add too much extra speed to compensate. The result is an arrival a few feet above the runway with a lot of extra airspeed. At that point, the pilot faces a dilemma: The speed must be dissipated for a proper landing or, as an alternative, the airplane must be flown onto the runway at a higher-than-normal speed. A great number of landing accidents in high wind conditions are associated with the choice of the latter method of landing.

What is a proper approach speed in gusty conditions? The normal approach speed plus the difference between the steady wind and the peak gust is a maximum. Any speed higher than that would have to be considered excessive. Some just add half the difference between the steady wind and the peak gust, and that is generally adequate except in extreme conditions.

How It's Done

How do pilots wreck airplanes after an approach at an excessive speed? One way is to run off the end of the runway, though if the wind is anything other than ninety degrees across the runway, the wind helps on cutting the required runway length after a fast approach. The more common way to bend the airplane comes after a crosswind landing in a tricycle-gear airplane with an improper distribution of weight on the wheels—meaning a concentration of weight on the nose rather than the main gear. In extreme cases, the nosewheel contacts the runway while the mains are still airborne. Nose gear assemblies tend to be less stout than the mains, and there's but one gear there whereas there are two at the rear. It is obvious that the main gear should take the brunt of anything and that doing it backward can only result in damage.

If the nose gear is subjected to enough abuse on landing, it will fail. Or it might maintain an outward appearance of health while the firewall, to which many nosewheels are attached, bends. Either event is expensive.

Wheelbarrowing

In instances where the nosewheel survives the initial on-slaught, the improper weight distribution on the wheels of a tricycle can still master the pilot. The phenomenon is called *wheelbarrowing*, and anyone who has ever crashed with an overloaded wheelbarrow knows how it works. The weight is forward and steering is difficult, if not impossible. With weight in a tricycle-gear airplane forward, the pivot point is at the front, and there's just no way to have much influence on where the airplane goes in such a situation. Steering is based on having weight on the rear wheels, and steering is very important in a crosswind.

A couple of items of technique can help minimize the risks in a crosswind touchdown and rollout.

First, use the minimum possible flap setting. That often means no flaps in some light airplanes. You can touch on the rear wheels first at a higher speed when flaps are not used, and control effectiveness will thus be better both before and after touchdown. This isn't applicable on very short airports, but if the runway is short and the crosswind strong, it is time to go somewhere else anyway. If the pilot's operating handbook does not specify an approach speed when flaps are not used, try 1.3 times the flaps-up stalling speed and then add an appropriate amount for gusts.

The other technique item is something to remember *not* to do. When landing in a crosswind (or at any time, for that matter), the thought should be that the elevator control is being brought aft. It should *not* be pushed forward once the airplane is close to the runway, in the landing process. If the airplane balloons up, just stop moving the wheel aft. Use a little power if the balloon is high, the airspeed is low, and the airplane feels as if it is about to develop a very high sink rate. But leave the elevator alone until the airplane is back close to the runway, then start working on the aft movement again. Charging the mind with such a thought will keep you away from a porpoising situation where the airplane might contact the runway and bounce, and bounce, and bounce, with the pilot moving the elevator control out of phase with the bounces and concentrating the force of contact on the nosewheel each time. Such maneuvers tend to get worse instead of better and go on to a conclusion. (The only exception to this is in a wheel landing in a conventional gear airplane, where the wheel must be moved forward at the moment of touchdown.)

Go Around?

Fortunately, landing accidents are not often serious. The situation can, however, become serious if the pilot does not exercise a measure of discipline and resist any temptation to go around late in an attempted landing.

There are two prime reasons a pilot might elect to go around. If the crosswind seems like it is more than might be manageable as the airplane is flared a few feet above the runway, it can prompt thoughts about going around. So can excessive use of runway for the slowing process before landing. There is, however, a point beyond which a go-around shouldn't be attempted. It is good to stake out that point early in the approach. On my home airport (single north/south runway, 3,000 feet long with a taxiway a few hundred feet south of the midpoint), I approach in strong crosswinds with the firm resolve to go around if the rear wheels are not firmly on the ground when passing the taxiway on a north landing or a few hundred feet before the taxiway on a south landing. (That is for light airplanes; in a twin the point would be much sooner.) If, after landing, it appeared that a stop wouldn't be possible, that would be tough. I'd just stay down and go on off the end.

The hazard in a late go-around is precisely the same as the hazard in a marginal takeoff with a strong crosswind, as covered in the discussion of wind effects on the departure phase of flight.

Sheared on Approach

Wind shear is an approach hazard that we all need to understand. The most common shear problem is created by a decreasing headwind component on final. It is not uncommon to find strong winds, thirty knots or more, at 1,000 or 2,000 feet with the wind nearly calm at the surface. As the airplane descends, it is not in a steady wind and the airspeed will be affected.

Wind shear effect on airspeed is a bit hard to grasp, with perhaps the best rationalization coming from a comparison of groundspeed and airspeed. If the airspeed is ninety knots on final and the airplane is flying with a thirty-knot headwind as it descends through 1,000 feet, the groundspeed will be sixty knots. Simple. Now shear means the wind abruptly changes direction or velocity—with altitude in this example. Imagine that the wind drops to almost zero at 500 feet. As the airplane continues its descent from 1,000 feet, the airspeed remains on ninety and the groundspeed stays at sixty. Then the airplane moves rather quickly into the level where the wind is calm. At that level, the groundspeed would become ninety knots, the same as the airspeed, right? Right, but not immediately. The airplane's groundspeed was sixty knots as it descended from the thirty-knot headwind into the calm wind, and there's no way the airplane can instantly accelerate thirty knots. Instead, the airspeed decays to try and match the groundspeed.

Light airplanes accelerate rapidly in such a situation, and you'd certainly not see a full thirty-knot sag in airspeed. The encounter is usually felt as somewhat of a sink-ing spell, with a drop in airspeed noted. The seat of our pants tells us to add power to arrest the sink rate and help the decaying airspeed. This usually suffices. (In heavy airplanes, especially jets, acceleration is slower and wind shear can have much more serious consequences.)

Reverse the situation and fly with a diminishing tailwind. There the airspeed will tend to build, and the airplane will feel almost buoyant. Using the values in the preceding example, except changing the 30-knot headwind to a 30-knot tailwind, the groundspeed would be 120 knots as the airplane descends into the calm wind and the airspeed would try to match that momentarily. This sounds like free beer—nothing to worry about—but it can also create a hazard, an overshoot.

Example

An ILS approach at Sioux Falls, S.D., one winter day stands out as a prime example of the decreasing tailwind. The ILS there is to the northeast. The wind 2,000 feet above the ground was westerly and very strong, probably around thirty-five knots. From the outer marker to the runway the strong tailwind component would turn into a crosswind because the surface wind was southeasterly and rather fresh.

As I descended, my Skyhawk just did not want to stay on the glideslope. It was trending high, and for quite a while, perhaps as long as thirty seconds, I had the power off and was tracking the glideslope at a rather high airspeed. It was quite turbulent in clouds, too, another characteristic of wind shear.

Such a situation creates its problem after the airplane moves into the new wind situation. As the wind was changing and the airplane was adapting to the new situation, I was just about in a power-off dive. At some point, that would have to change back to a normal approach. That's no problem in a Skyhawk if anticipated—change the pitch attitude, add some power, and presto, everything is okay. In a heavier airplane, though, it would be possible to bomb right through the glideslope and into the ground if the changing situation were not anticipated. It is interesting, I think, that in quite a number of premature arrivals by air carrier aircraft the airplane was initially high on the glideslope. A correction was made to return the aircraft to the glideslope, but the correction was either excessive or flown for too long and the aircraft descended through the glideslope and into the ground.

How?

How do we know of wind shear so that we might make allowance for it? Beware of any situation where there is a marked difference in surface wind and wind aloft. And watch it when operating in a frontal zone or when flying in the vicinity of a thunderstorm. These are the situations most likely to create classic wind shear situations. Any strong and gusty wind condition can create localized wind shear that will affect the airplane momentarily.

The air carrier accidents related to wind shear are well documented. Airliners fly with flight recorders that show changes in airspeed as well as g-forces and other values. There is more guesswork to general aviation accidents, and there are probably a number of accidents in which wind shear is at least a contributing factor but isn't mentioned in the accident report because the investigators don't really have any after-the-fact means to pinpoint the possibility.

Wind, be it steady, gusty, or of the shear variety, is something to respect but not to fear. It affects takeoff performance, bounces the airplane around, and can induce variations to the approach and landing that we'd perhaps rather do without. Any reasonable wind-related risk is manageable, though. A pilot must only stay proficient at flying in wind, anticipate the effects, and fly with a cool head.

5 | The Stall/Spin

Back in the good old days, when airplanes were toys and the stall and cruising speeds were within a breath of one another, the stall/spin accident reigned supreme. Then came faster airplanes that were truly useful for flying across the country. The travel capability of these machines quickly outstripped the weather capability of pilots, and weather-related accidents moved to the forefront. In recent years, though, the pendulum seems to be swinging back a bit toward the stall/spin.

One positive note can be related to this. The accident rate has been improving slowly and steadily, and if the stall/spin has become a larger proportion of the total, that means something else is showing marked improvement. This would have to be in the weather area—a direct result of more pilots moving into IFR operations.

The stall/spin accident is deceptively simple. It involves only the pilot not letting the airplane fly. It can thus be subjeced to black-and-white discussion. Stalls are not like weather, where the go/no-go decision can be as fuzzy around the edges as early morning fog. They are not like night flying, where it can be technically VFR but practically IFR. And they are not like wind, where you might have a self-imposed wind limit of thirty knots and have to rationalize a situation where it's twenty-five gusting to thirty-five. A stall is a stall. The airplane is or is not in a stalled condition. And if provoked into a spin, there is no doubt about that condition of flight, no doubt at all.

Pet Theories

There are plenty of pet theories on stall/spin accidents. Some feel that most happen as the pilot makes that last turn in the pattern, from base to final. Others cite the departure phase of flight, especially from short fields. And a bunch of stall/spin accidents happen as a pilot maneuvers after a power failure. All those areas are strong factors, but something else leads the pack. About 40 percent of the stall/spin accidents occur away from the airport with the airplane functioning normally in a mechanical sense. Buzzing, aerobatics, and low passes are the prime producers of this type of accident.

Buzzing

In studying stall/spin accidents that occur when pilots become playful, plenty of similarities develop. The people involved tend to be students or relatively inexperienced private pilots. The airplanes are of the variety most often used for training. This is logical. There is no way a new pilot can take the airplane home to show the neighbors—no way, that is, other than through the medium of low-altitude flight. The temptation to do this is often strong—and fatal. Some buzzing accidents do involve more experienced pilots, and when this is the case, the buzz job is usually embellished with low-level aerobatics.

A buzzing accident is rather easy to dismiss: The pilot let his ego take command and he busted his tail. No sympathy can be generated for anyone other than passengers and survivors in such a case. The element of risk is obvious; the pilot elects to take the risk and then can't handle it. Of far more interest is the stall/spin that occurs away from the airport as a pilot is flying normally, or at least as the pilot is operating within the framework of the rules.

Training Flights

A number of airplanes spin to the ground during training flights. These are usually solo flights, the purpose of which was stall practice. The scenario is logical: A student pulls the airplane up into a stall, mishandles it at the stall, spins the airplane, and then does not do the proper things to recover from the spin. In most cases, the airplane is one that is certified for spins, so recovery should have been no problem. We will explore that later.

There are also some stall/spin training accidents involving instructors. For the most part, these involve airplanes that are not certificated for spins but that are spun for one reason or another. Certainly it is foolish to intentionally spin an airplane that isn't certificated for the maneuver because the reason spins aren't approved is usually related to poor recovery characteristics. That is more than enough reason not to spin one just for kicks. The rules basically say that in single-engine airplanes not certificated for spins the manufacturer must demonstrate recovery from a one-turn spin in not more than one additional turn. There is no spin requirement for the certification of light twins. Anyone who spins past one turn in a single that isn't certificated for spins or spins a twin at all has suddenly assumed the role of experimental test pilot. No experimental test pilot would spin such an airplane at all without a parachute and a quick release door on the airplane. Most would also want a spin chute at the tail of the airplane to facilitate recovery from a flat spin.

Other Reasons

Some pilots spin-in away from the airport for other reasons. In a sample of accidents, a twin had an engine failure while

IFR and was subsequently seen spinning out of the bottom of the clouds. Two engines didn't do that pilot much good. The entire twin question will be discussed in chapter 8, but this is an example of the problems caused by a combination of asymmetric thrust and a stall. There are also numerous stall/spin accidents after the engine fails in a single. These will be separated from en route stall/spin accidents as well as those occurring during normal arrivals because of the different nature of the situation. They will also be discussed in chapter 8.

There are many stall/spin accidents around the airport. In most every case, there is an extenuating circumstance that helps the pilot back himself into a corner. On departure perhaps the airplane is overloaded, the density altitude high, or the airport short. Some of the departure stall/spin accidents involve engine malfunctions during initial climb, usually for pilot-induced reasons such as fuel system mismanagement, and where there is serious trouble it is often related to an attempted power-off turn back toward the airport at low altitude.

On approaches there might be an occasional problem during a normal turn from base to final, but this is rare enough almost not to mention. Horsing around leads to some stall/spins during the approach, as pilots try to enjoy steep turns while maneuvering in the pattern. Others come when lining up on final is made difficult because of a nonstandard pattern induced by other traffic or because of a downwind condition on base leg that causes an overshoot of the turn onto final.

Flaps

It is possible to link some stall/spin accidents to flaps or to
the pilot's misunderstanding of the flaps. A go-around is the
most likely place to find trouble because of this. Some airplanes will just barely fly level with full flaps, even at full
power, so there is an apparent need to retract flaps early in
a go-around. Retraction of flaps raises the stalling speed,
though, and this must be recognized when retracting flaps
in a tedious situation. A lot of simulated go-around drill
during training or checkout is good preventive action. The
trim changes that accompany the retraction of flaps can
then be anticipated when the chips are down, as can the
effect of flaps on stalling speed or lift. On a Skyhawk, for
example, the first ten degrees of flaps lowers the stalling
speed by almost five knots. Going from ten degrees onto
full forty degrees of flaps lowers the stalling speed only an
additional three knots. In a pinch you would be getting rid
of a lot of drag while accepting a small increase in stalling
speed by retracting flaps from forty to ten degrees, but in
retracting from ten to zero, it would be a matter of increasing the stalling speed quite a bit for a slight decrease in
drag. The practice area is a good place to see, feel, and
explore this.

It's Logical

The factors found in stall/spin accidents, whether they happen around or away from airports, are logical enough. We can study the times, places, and circumstances and say, "Yes, old Joe spun in because. . . ." We know that the stalling speed increases with angle of bank, for example, and the relationship between this and stall/spin accidents is made clear by the fact that accidental spins often start in turns. What is not logical is the lack of pilot discipline involved in such accidents. Surely every pilot is aware of the seriousness of flying in a manner that increases the risk of a stall at low altitude or a spin that flattens into an unrecoverable mode and of arrival at the ground in any kind of spin. Every pilot, too, is aware of how you stall an airplane. There's no way to do it without increasing the wing's angle of attack to the stalling angle. By the same token, a reduction in angle of attack will, if done at the proper time, preclude a stall or entry into a spin.

Poor Portrayal

My opinion is that what is taught in training today does not always portray the stall/spin problem as it exists. For example, in stall recovery the emphasis is on putting the nose on the horizon and applying full power. This often works quite well, but it is not always realistic. Why? Because power (or additional power) is not available in a high percentage of the situations that lead to stall/spin accidents. In departure accidents the engine is generally operating at full power to begin with. There is no way to add power. If the problem is engine failure on takeoff for whatever reason, we have no power to add. The buzzing stall/spin accidents generally come with the engine roaring—you sure don't buzz to be quiet. Some of the spins in training can be related to not reducing power instead of not applying it. (Cutting the power is a prime requirement in spin recovery in most airplanes.) The only place where the use of power might really help is in moving away from the stall on approach. And then this is only true if power is available. Remember, many of those approach stalls come during forced landings when no power is available.

Reduce Angle of Attack

Might it not be better to develop a strong understanding of angle of attack and think in terms of reducing angle of attack—wheel or stick forward—as *the* means of stall recovery or avoidance? Power, if available, can be used as a secondary item to help the airspeed move up and to minimize altitude loss. But if the mind is to be charged with a useful, all-purpose plan in case of trouble, it would have to be related to angle-of-attack reduction with the elevator—something that is always available.

The Angle

Angle of attack is the single most important thing to understand when contemplating the stall/spin accident. What is angle of attack? It is basically the difference between where the wing is pointed and where the wing is going. At cruise the wing is about level and the airplane is going ahead; the angle is very small. Pull the nose up to a thirty-degree angle above the horizon, and initially the angle of attack remains small as the airplane zooms upward, climbing and dissipating speed. As the airplane slows, the angle of attack starts increasing rapidly if you hold the nose at that thirty-degree angle. The increase can be seen by comparing the vertical speed indication with the nose-up pitch attitude. When the nose is first pulled up, there is a lot of rate of climb: The airplane is pointed up and it is going up. Then the rate of climb begins decaying even though the nose is held high. That is evidence of increasing angle of attack. The vertical speed will be down close to zero as the airplane stalls.

Zoom

In a buzzing accident a pilot might pull into such a thirty-degree nose-up attitude in a last and dramatic zoom. Or the nose might be pulled higher than thirty degrees above the horizon. Speed dissipates, and by the time it's down to a value that might alarm the pilot, the airplane could be more or less committed to disaster. The pilot might look at the airspeed and see it on a reasonable value when well into the zoom, giving a false feeling of well-being. The angle of attack might be increasing so rapidly at that point, though, that it will reach the stalling angle even after the pilot begins to reduce back pressure in an effort to reduce angle of attack. If the pilot had mentally compared the nose-up pitch angle with the full power stalling angle, though, the pilot would have noted that the difference exceeded the stalling angle of attack—a sure indication of impending trouble.

The Insidious Stall

Such an ending is reserved for those who buzz. Of more concern is the insidious stall, the one that bites a pilot who is trying to maneuver an airplane for a purpose: to get over, around, or safely down. The part about angle of attack is equally important here, but it is more difficult to see.

Set the stage with a descending left turn. As the airplane is banked, back pressure must be held on the stick or wheel to keep the nose from dropping. A little is fine, but recognize a message: The nose wants to be lower in a turn because the airplane is trying to seek the same angle of attack it was trimmed for in level flight. The airplane is trying to protect itself. By adding back pressure, the pilot is increasing the angle of attack, cutting the margin between the actual and the stalling angle. As you hold back pressure in a turn, you are resisting the airplane's desire to protect itself (and you). In normal turns this is a necessary action if altitude is to be maintained, and it is perfectly safe. It's a different matter when low and slow.

Now we are in a thirty-degree banked descending turn. Drag increases as g-load builds and angle of attack increases. The rate of descent will increase. The eye might perceive this increased closure rate with the ground as being undesirable and send a message to the brain to do something about it. If the brain suffers from the illusion that the elevator control is an absolute controller of up and down, of altitude, the solution might be to add some more back pressure.

Turn Faster

Meanwhile, perhaps the turn is not progressing satisfactorily. How do you make the airplane turn faster? More bank, which will further decrease the gap between actual and the stalling angle of attack, or a touch of rudder to skid the airplane around to the new heading a bit more swiftly. Choose rudder? Carry on—it helps promote the type of problem we are discussing.

The addition of rudder in the direction of turn tends to make the airplane want to bank more steeply. It is called *overbanking,* and the obvious solution is a bit of aileron in the opposite direction, to the right in case of our left turn.

The stage is almost set, so pause for a moment to reflect

on the basic cause of a spin. One wing stalls while the other one is flying and becomes more deeply stalled than the other wing as things progress. Yaw is the best medium for this. What better way to generate yaw at the stall than a skidding turn? In our case, the right wing is flying faster than the left wing. The left wing's angle of attack is at 16.5 degrees now; the right isn't so precariously near the stall.

All the controls are still working to some extent as the turn continues. Pull back on the wheel a little more in a misguided attempt to arrest the rate of sink. A little more left rudder to speed the turn. And a little more right aileron to combat the overbanking. The rate of sink increases more, and the bank suddenly steepens precipitously. The time has come. The left wing reaches its stalling angle of attack and gives up. The right wing is still playful and keeps trying to fly.

The event develops into a spin from the bottom of a turn. The airplane spins to the left from a left turn. This is a rather sudden maneuver in most airplanes, one in which the airplane goes vertical or even slightly inverted as it falls off into the spin. Even if recovery is instituted immediately, a substantial amount of altitude will likely be lost. If it happens low to the ground, someone's nose is going to be muddied.

The Keys

A lot of things warn when this is about to happen. One key is back pressure. The pilot is pulling back on the wheel, no doubt about that. Too much pull should be a warning. The opposite aileron to combat overbanking should be a warning, too. Anytime it takes a considerable amount of opposite aileron to keep the airplane from exceeding the desired angle of bank it is time to reduce the angle of attack. It is also time to check the slip and skid indicator (ball), because it'll probably tell the tale on skid in the direction of bank—a suggestion that you get your foot off the bottom rudder.

A spin from the bottom of a turn would most likely come as the airplane is being maneuvered for landing, or as it is being turned at low altitude immediately after takeoff or for the purpose of circling something on the ground.

Mirage

The visual illusion in a power-off, or low-power approach, might be one of already having the nose down below the horizon. Thus, putting the nose on the horizon and adding power for recovery would not be applicable, as you'd have to increase angle of attack to accomplish that. Angle of attack can be at the stalling level even with the nose down; all it takes is the difference between where the wing is pointed and where it is going. This is most pronounced in turns.

In the Beginning

Even during initial climb, the nose is not likely very high as the airplane approaches a problem. When we practice stalls at altitude, the approach to the stall is from an airspeed above the stall. The nose is high because we had to put it there to dissipate speed. In a departure situation the approach to the stall is from a low airspeed, and as often as not the problem is in failing to obtain airspeed rather than failing to maintain it.

Elusive Horizon

The horizon is often elusive during departure. The tops of trees ahead do not likely represent the horizon, and if the terrain slopes upward or there is a mountain in the distance, the horizon can be difficult, if not impossible, to determine. In such a situation, what you feel and what you see on the instrument panel in the way of attitude and airspeed indications must be the governing factors. If there is doubt about getting over the trees or clearing an obstruction, pulling back on the wheel to make a staggering airplane go up is just not the ticket.

Ailerons

The role of the ailerons in stall/spin accidents must be further contemplated because the improper use of ailerons in some airplanes can actually lead to a spin—even with the rudder centered. And the role of ailerons is directly related to difficulty in spin recovery by a pilot not familiar with spins.

As noted, yaw at the moment of stall is what makes an airplane spin. Some airplanes tend to stall and fall through straight ahead; others don't. When one doesn't, the cause is either poor rigging or just the basic design of the airplane. If the ailerons alone are used in an attempt to keep the wings level in a stall or to keep the airplane from overbanking as it reaches the stall in a turn, some airplanes can be provoked to spin simply by that use of ailerons as the airplane stalls.

Adverse Yaw

Remember adverse yaw? For example, move the wheel to the right and note that the nose of the aircraft swings a bit to the left as it rolls into a right turn. There is more drag on the lowered aileron than on the raised one. That phenomenon is more pronounced at the stall, as the flow separates from the top of the wing and the upward deflected aileron loses its bite. So if the airplane rolls to the left at the stall and you apply full right aileron, the effect will be to intensify the yaw to the left. The lowered left aileron does it. The lowered aileron also serves the purpose of demanding that wing to generate some lift to come back to level. That also promotes the stall. More up than down aileron travel minimizes this on most airplanes. The spinproof Ercoupe of a few decades ago had the ultimate aileron guard against the spin: Its roll control was virtually accomplished with up aileron only. When the wheel was full right, for example, the right aileron would be all the way up and the left one almost flush.

New World

Once in an aileron-induced spin, a pilot is in a strange new world. The entry into a spin is quick and disorienting. A pilot's first thought is related to what is going on; many pilots do not realize it is a spin. Rather, they think something is basically wrong with the flying machine. The control wheel might be full back and to the right, yet the airplane is pointed straight down and is rotating to the left. The correct recovery procedure for most airplanes is to neutralize the wheel, in both roll and pitch. If that is done quickly, it's probably enough; the airplane will at that moment make the transition from spin to dive. If this fails to stop the spin, rudder would be required to stop the rotation as the wheel is moved to a neutral position. But it is not easy to move the wheel forward and to the left when the airplane is going madly down and to the left. That is why some student pilots spin all the way to the ground from a respectable altitude after accidentally spinning an airplane. The proper recovery action is so unnatural that their minds simply can't make the hands do the necessary work. And even when a recovery is instituted promptly, almost 1,000 feet can be lost in a spin, especially one from the bottom of a turn.

Spin recovery problems can also come when a pilot fails to close the throttle in an accidental spin. Power tends to make a spin flatten, and once an airplane is in a flat spin the sure method of recovery becomes parachute-related.

Solutions

It is easier to find fault with today's methods of stall practice than it is to suggest great new ways to look at the problem. The only realistic way to simulate the insidious stall at low altitude would be to do stalls at low altitude. That would create more problems than it might solve. The real solutions are probably in individual understanding of the situations in which stall/spin accidents occur—buzzing, unwarranted low flying, and low slow turns—and avoidance of those things. The indications of an impending problem should be mentally filed for reference, too. The portents of trouble are a lot of back pressure held on the wheel or a lot of aileron against a turn. Rapidly decaying airspeed is also a warning, as is a substantial angular difference between where the airplane is pointed and where it will really

go with the power selected. These are all things to understand and be wary of.

Another important item is the use of rudder. Back in the
good old days, it was taught that the rudder is the one
control that is effective through the stall. Rudder controls
yaw, so the rudder and the rudder alone can be used to
keep the airplane from spinning as the airplane stalls. This
was often demonstrated in what was called a "complete"
stall. The drill was to stall the airplane and keep it stalled,
keeping the wheel or stick full aft until the nose dropped
through the horizon. The aileron would remain centered,
and the rudder would be used to keep the wings level. It
was good exercise and a good demonstration. The airplanes
of the day (Cubs, Aeroncas, and the like) were good spin-
ners and would often reward a poor effort with a spin.
Also, for the pilot who didn't believe that ailerons could
cause an airplane to spin, a convincer was to keep the stick
back and the airplane stalled while trying to keep the wings
level with the ailerons instead of with the rudder. Got a lot
of spins out of that.

In Your Hand

Foremost, though, is an understanding of what the elevators of an airplane really do. They control angle of attack, not up and down, not altitude. Many accidental spins
are probably related to a strong notion that the elevators
control altitude—pull back to go up. That doesn't work

when the chips are down. Angle of attack is the key to the stall, and the elevators are the key to angle of attack. Always think in terms of reducing angle of attack: wheel or stick forward when the airplane begins feeling squirrelly.

Spin Lesson?

The increasing incident of stall/spin accidents has rekindled the controversy over whether or not spins should be demonstrated or taught to all pilots. Certainly it can be argued that spin training might help in the instances where a student spins an airplane at altitude and never recovers. And it has always seemed a good idea at least to demonstrate spins to pilots flying airplanes that are easily spinnable.

But if we are to have a requirement for spins then the airplane builders will be forced to build airplanes that are easy to spin. If they are easy to spin intentionally, they might also be easy to spin accidentally. This might be counterproductive. The best thing to do in relation to spinning would be to build airplanes that are difficult to spin— accidentally or on purpose.

6 | A Weighty Subject

The morning paper said only that the airplane had crashed while taking off, and that two people were dead and two critically injured. No details. It happened at a friend's airport—a rather small grass strip—and I started to call him but decided against it. He might be busy, and I could find out more later. As I was thinking about it, he telephoned to ask me to come have a look and talk with him about the accident. It made two of a kind at his airport (over a long period of time), and he was concerned.

The airstrip is 2,200 feet long, grass, manicured like a golf green, and it was resplendent in sparkling sunshine as I rounded the bend in the river to land downwind. The approaches are better that way, and it would take at least

100

ten knots of wind to urge an upwind landing from over the obstructions. The accident of the day before happened as the pilot took off toward those obstructions with four people in a four-place airplane. The airport is well within the capability of most light airplanes (I've seen a King Air use it with no problems), but it is a field that requires care and thought. Certainly there is nothing wrong with this. Not every runway in the land can be 5,000 feet long with clear approaches.

After I landed, the airport owner told me about the accident. The FAA and NTSB people had already done their work and left. There were enough facts and there had been enough witnesses, all with about the same observations, for the Feds to write the accident up and go away.

Over Gross

In addition to having four men and 183 pounds of baggage on board, the pilot elected to fill the fuel tanks. The investigators computed the actual takeoff weight to be approximately 200 pounds over gross. If all the baggage was in the baggage compartment, the center of gravity would have been outside the aft limits. The airplane manual suggests the use of flaps for short field takeoffs, but witnesses reported that flaps were not used. There was a gusty crosswind.

The airplane must have become airborne about two-thirds of the way down the runway. Almost immediately after lift-off, the pilot apparently elected to abort the take-

off. The visual picture at such a point would have suggested
a very difficult situation at best if the airplane was not flying
eagerly.

Witnesses did not agree on where the airplane touched
back down, and the only tire marks in the grass were a few
hundred feet past the official end of the runway, still on
level and smooth turf but very near the rough. The airplane
was still on runway heading as it passed near a house and
moved between two trees, shearing both wing tips. The next
obstructions were much less friendly. Reacting to the upcoming trees and deep gully, the pilot must have pulled the
wheel back because it appeared that the airplane struck two
very substantial trees while about five or six feet in the air
in quite a nose-high attitude. One tree got the left wing
about a third of the way out toward the tip. The left side of
the nose struck the other tree: There was wood imbedded
in the left front cylinder, and pieces of engine baffle were
imbedded in the tree.

The airplane was probably moving at from fifty to sixty
knots at impact. The left wing stopped at the tree, but its
gas tank was flung to the other side of the gully. Some part
of the left front side of the fuselage stopped, but the heavy
parts continued on. The instrument panel was down in the
gully, the engine was on the other side, and the nose gear
was beyond the engine. The right wing was down in the
gully, and the cabin door and the floor of the forward cabin
were still loosely attached to the right wing. The right front
seat was still on the floor by the door. The forward fuselage
was completely shattered, but the aft fuselage, from about
two-thirds of the way back in the cabin, stopped at the trees
and remained relatively intact. The rear seats did not stay

in place as the cabin floor came apart. The baggage and the people came to rest down in the gully. The survivors were in the rear seats.

Thought-Provoking

Accident sites are both sad and thought-provoking. The thought of an airplane being transformed into such a mess in a split second is difficult to accept. The thought that people lost their lives as it happened is unhappy at best. And the concept of an intelligent and successful person stacking the unfavorable odds by overloading an airplane on a relatively small airport is one of the perplexing, recurring, and hard-to-understand phenomena of general aviation.

With full fuel the flight would have been nonstop to home base. This must have had some bearing on the pilot's decision to fill it up. Nobody knows why the pilot did not select takeoff flaps or why the runway with the worst obstructions was selected.

A lesson, a tragic lesson. Some might point a finger at the beautiful airstrip—idyllic, waiting for people to realize the true potential of an airplane by flying to where they want to go. Some might point a finger at the little airplane; it killed, it is a villain. Not true. What is true is that the airstrip, and airplanes in general, are unforgiving of many types of basic errors. Meanwhile, the trees survive, growing slowly and patiently. The pieces of metal imbedded in the trunk will probably stay there. If a pilot tempted with overloading would only look at that tree before doing so, it would teach a lesson silently, painlessly, and at no cost. If the lesson couldn't be learned the easy way, the tree stands ready to teach it the hard way, again and again.

NTSB Report

In a pamphlet discussing weight and balance as a safety consideration, the National Transportation Safety Board notes 213 related accidents in the U.S. during a five-year period. The 213 accidents resulted in 273 fatalities and 115 serious injuries, which underlines the fact that these accidents tend to be serious when they do occur. The NTSB report gave a number of examples, and it is noteworthy that in virtually every case at least one other factor combined with the overload or imbalance to make a difficult situation impossible, as was the case in the accident just described. One pilot attempted takeoff in an overloaded airplane at a density altitude of 9,800 feet. Another overloaded his airplane and crashed while attempting an uphill takeoff at a density altitude of 3,000 feet. A light airplane that was 244 pounds over gross crashed while attempting a takeoff on a very hot day. A twin crashed shortly after encountering icing conditions following an overweight takeoff.

CG

Those were primarily related to weight; there are numerous accidents with center-of-gravity connections, too.

When trouble comes, the center of gravity is usually aft of the limit, and the flight usually ends in a stall/spin because this condition affects the longitudinal stability of an airplane. In severe cases of aft CG, the nose of an airplane pitches up and continues up until the airplane stalls, even though the pilot applies full forward elevator—a very unpleasant thought.

Of the two limitations, weight and CG, weight offers the most temptations. Rare is the airplane that can carry full fuel, full seats, and full baggage. And while most users seldom have need to do all those things simultaneously, the need does occasionally arise to extract that much utility from the airplane. Ironically, that need seems to present itself on smaller airports more often than not. The smaller airports tend to be used more during recreational flights, when the load factor is highest. Take as many people as possible to the fun spot, and don't leave any gear behind. To compound the problem, add the heat of summer, when recreational flying is at its peak, to prolong the takeoff run and cut the rate of climb.

Rate of Climb

Next, consider that rate of climb is the item which most often sets the gross weight limit of light airplanes. The regulations require that an airplane climb at sea level, in standard conditions, 11.5 times the stalling speed (in knots) with takeoff power, the gear extended in the case of a retractable, and with takeoff flaps. The fact that rate of climb is the airplane's tender spot in relation to weight makes it logical that most accidents involving overloaded airplanes happen during initial climb.

For example, consider a 150-horsepower Cessna Skyhawk with a 230-pound (10 percent) overload condition on a ninety-degree day at 2,500 feet elevation. The airplane's normal rate of climb in standard conditions is 645 feet per minute. The temperature and elevation cuts that to 480 feet per minute. The overload slices that 480 down to 384 feet per minute. (The effect of overloading on performance is twice the percentage over gross. In this example 10 percent over means 20 percent less climb.) The angle of climb speed increases to sixty-three knots, and the result is a rather flat climb. (Performance speeds—stall, climb, and maneuvering—change at a rate approximately half the percentage over or under gross weight. For 10 percent over, add 5 percent to the climb speed in this example.) A downdraft or some turbulence might, in fact, make the rate of climb less than the amount necessary to climb 1 foot for each 20 feet of forward motion. That is rather critical because the obstruction criteria for VFR runways calls for a 20:1 slope. (All runways do not meet this slope requirement.)

In most weight-related accidents the pilot could in fact take the information in the aircraft manual and the rules of thumb just given to determine the effects of overloading and see on paper that the proposed mission is impossible. This is certainly a sensible precaution to take if there is any doubt.

Structure

An overload also compromises the airplane's structural strength, but this doesn't appear as the cause of great problems. I can't remember a single accident in which an overloaded airplane failed when operated within airspeed limits, though there might have been some. There are instances of overloaded airplanes failing after the pilot lost control in adverse weather conditions, but in these instances the airplane would likely have broken regardless of the weight.

The reason airplanes don't break when overloaded is because they are quite strong. Again using a Skyhawk at 10 percent over gross as an example, the limit load factor drops only from 3.8 to 3.45 G's. That is a far less catastrophic change than the 20-percent increase in takeoff distance, 20-percent decrease in rate of climb, and greater-than-20-percent decrease in climb gradient. We almost never even get close to the limit load factor of an airplane, but on those hot and short strips we are often very close to situations where the maximum rate of climb is required to get the airplane up and over the obstacles.

Don't Misunderstand

That is not meant to condone overloading when runway length isn't a consideration. Overloading does cut the structural margin, and thus it shouldn't be done. Another likely problem caused by an overload is engine overheating as the airplane struggles to lift the weight.

In a sense the pilot becomes an experimental test pilot when an airplane is overloaded because the airplane is being asked to perform outside the envelope it was subjected to in testing. Even so it is sometimes hard to argue with the pilot who overloads an airplane slightly to avoid a fuel problem at the end of a flight if the departure runway is long and surface temperatures are not high. The rationale in such a situation might be that the compromise in climb and structural strength will affect the safety of the flight only slightly, whereas a compromise in the fuel load will affect the safety of the flight substantially. It can be a tough decision, but the right answer has to be the legal answer: Pick an airplane that will fly legally with both the desired fuel and payload and stay within the weight limits.

There should be no temptation on exceeding the center-of-gravity limits of an airplane because controllability becomes the question with CG. There are no formulas to use in illustrating what exceeding the limit a given amount might cause. The aft limit is the critical one and must be considered an absolute. The forward CG limit is usually based on landing considerations. The airplane must have enough elevator effectiveness to land on the main wheels first at full-forward CG.

Spin recovery is one factor setting the aft CG limit on

most single-engine airplanes. As noted, a single-engine airplane must recover from a one-turn spin in not more than one additional turn, and manufacturers have been known to lose experimental airplanes in spins as they attempt to move the CG limit aft. When it gets too far aft, the spin flattens before one turn is completed, the test pilot has to use his parachute, and the aft CG limit of the airplane is moved forward.

Longitudinal stability also deteriorates as the CG moves aft, and if the airplane is loaded far enough aft, the airplane ceases to have positive longitudinal stability. An airplane becomes difficult to fly when it reaches this point, where virtually no force on the wheel is required to change pitch attitude. In an extreme case the nose of the aircraft just pitches up, and up, and keeps on going up until the airplane stalls, even with the elevator control full forward.

Examples

Two examples illustrate the potential of aft CG operation.

A twin was taking off with the CG far aft, and as the gear retracted (moving the CG back even more because of aft retraction), the nose of the aircraft started to pitch up. The nose-up trend continued until the aircraft stalled. Might the pilot have salvaged things by putting the gear back down? It is possible.

In another, a pilot had flown an airplane extensively for a number of years on the same type of mission, with the CG slightly aft of the limit on almost all flights. The airplane always did require quite a bit of nose-down trim, but he had no problem until the trim tab control rod broke, making trim unavailable. The pilot reported that it was barely within his physical capability to keep the nose of the aircraft from pitching up into a stall. The return and landing was successful but touchy.

Experience Doesn't Help

It is interesting that commercial and airline transport-rated pilots were involved in almost 60 percent of the weight-and-balance-related accidents in a four-year period. Perhaps this suggests that experience prompts a pilot to feel immune to the effects of excessive weight or of exceeding the center-of-gravity limits. Whatever, it proves once again that the laws of gravity and aerodynamics don't make exceptions based on pilot experience.

Density Altitude

High density altitude often figures in weight-related accidents. It is important to note also that density altitude can be a factor in accidents where weight and balance are within limits. Pilots of Part 25 aircraft, air carriers and

bizjets for the most part, must calculate the distance required for every takeoff, and required performance param-
eters must be met for every takeoff. This often requires that
the airplanes be flown from high and hot airports at weights
below gross. We don't have to meet this requirement in
most general aviation operations, and many pilots feel that
as long as the gross weight is not exceeded, everything will
be okay. This is an erroneous assumption. The situation
often arises, especially in high and hot country, where the
only safe weight is one below gross weight.

Mountain Flying

Mountain flying is a separate subject, best learned through
dual instruction from an experienced mountain instructor
before tackling the Rockies in a light airplane. One thing
does stand out in the accidents that flatlanders have in the
mountains, though: Any problem usually stems either from
a disregard of the effects of wind over the mountains and
the rule of thumb to stay out of the mountains when the
wind at ridge levels is forecast in excess of thirty knots or
from density altitude problems.

Those of us who are used to flying where field elevations
are below a couple of thousand feet need to carefully rethink our situation before takeoff at a high altitude airport,
as well as before heading across high terrain. The airplane
knows only density altitude. Just because the specs say the
airplane's ceiling is 13,500 feet, that does not mean the

airplane will climb to that altitude on the altimeter. If it is eighty-three degrees at the Leadville, Colorado, airport (elevation 9,927), your 13,500-foot service ceiling airplane would be at its service ceiling while resting on the runway because that's about what the density altitude would be under the existing conditions. The only way to fly would be to lighten the load. (The same thing is often true at short airports.)

By the same token, a pilot flying an airplane with a 13,500-foot service ceiling wouldn't stand a chance of making it across an 11,000-foot ridge on a hot day at gross weight because the density altitude of the ridge top might be above 13,500 feet.

High temperatures can have a profound influence on takeoff, climb, and service ceiling. Risk management must begin with careful calculations and continue throughout the flight with continuing calculations and no self-deception. For the takeoff a good rule is to require a runway length at least equal to the calculated distance to takeoff and climb to fifty feet. That gives some margin for error. Margin is very necessary because all takeoff figures are based on perfection, a maximum effort—full throttle before brake release, a new engine, standard conditions, a hard and level surface, and flawless flying technique. Factors are included to allow for things like grass and higher- (or lower-) than-standard temperatures and elevation, but there's nothing there to use in padding the number for an engine that's not as peppy as it used to be or for flying technique that's not exactly swift. We must add some for good measure, and the use of the "over fifty-foot" figure in setting the absolute minimum for actual runway length works well here. If obstructions are close to the end of the runway, an additional allowance would need to be made. In every case, it is good to off-load some fuel or cabin weight if there is any doubt.

The next thing would be to ascertain that the engine is indeed putting out an appropriate amount of power and to be satisfied with this either before releasing the brakes or very early in the takeoff run. If the airplane has a fixed-pitch prop, look at static rpm; with a constant speed check rpm and manifold pressure. Just the feel of initial acceleration can be a good indication in a familiar airplane, too.

Once the roll starts, it is wise to recognize that there is a point of no return on every takeoff. Up to that point, aborting the takeoff will cause no problem. Pull the power back, put on the brakes, and stop with the airplane and people in the same condition as at the start of the roll. Past that point the choice is between a successful flight and an accident. In studying reports on takeoff accidents from small airports, it is hard to believe that there wasn't usually strong doubt in the pilot's mind before the airplane passed the point of no return on the runway.

The farther a pilot goes past the point of no return on an impossible takeoff, the more serious the accident that follows. If an abort is attempted late, as in the example at the beginning of this chapter, the entry into the rough will be at high speed. If the pilot keeps trying, gets the airplane off, but strikes obstructions or stalls the airplane in an attempt to "make" it fly over obstructions, the consequences might also be very serious.

Again, the situation is very much in the hands of the pilot. The information is available to determine that a takeoff will or will not be successful. Hunches, wishes, eyeball estimates, and guesses don't count. It is cut and dried. The airplane has measurable performance, and the runway and obstructions are known quantities. And weight plays a key role.

Flying Technique

Even the flying technique involved in a takeoff is a methodical procedure that must be followed. In jet aircraft a careful determinaton of lift-off speed is made. We should do the same thing in light airplanes. Once the field length has been calculated as adequate, a plan for the takeoff would include the determination of the lift-off and the best angle-of-climb speeds. In a Skyhawk operating at gross weight, for example, the pilot's operating handbook calls for lifting the nosewheel at fifty-two knots and climbing at fifty-nine knots until obstacles are cleared. The performance figures are based on the use of those speeds. Make the calculations, fly the speeds with precision, and have confidence in the proceedings. If you don't make the calculations and guess at the proper speeds, what comes next is anybody's guess. A careful computation of weight, balance, and performance is as important to the safety of a flight as is the weather check and the preflight inspection.

7 | Midair Collisions

There is an old, true, and somewhat trite saying that a midair collision can spoil your whole day. The thought of a midair probably strikes more fear into the hearts of pilots and laymen than does the thought of any other aerial misadventure. Many pilots are even egotistical enough to profess aeronautical fear only of the midair. It is the one thing not completely under their control and is thus the only thing they fear might ever sneak up and bite. The layman's fear is of being in an airplane that is struck by another airplane, usually a small airplane that, in the mind of an airline passenger, "shouldn't be there." Then the fear is of falling from the sky in the crippled machine. It is this public fear that prompts Congress to appropriate billions a year for the purpose of air traffic control.

There is at least some basis for apprehension about mid-air collisions. Even in a year when there are no collisions involving air carriers, about 100 people, pilots and passengers, plus or minus 20 or 30, are involved in midair collisions in the United States. That number appears small when compared with the over 2,000 people involved in weather-related accidents, but it must be considered significant because it couples with a basic human fear.

Many Survive

A myth to puncture quickly is the one about your being automatically wiped out if involved in a midair collision. In fact, 60 to 65 percent of the people who are involved in midair collisions survive. That doesn't advertise it as an appealing new outdoor sport, but it does add perspective. This number is almost equal to the percentage who survive weather-related accidents, some of which are relatively simple encounters with wind or density altitude, and it is in excess of the percentage of participants who survive stall/spin accidents. The midair collision thus must be positioned as a general aviation accident type only about equal in severity, though not, of course, in frequency, to the two biggies, weather and stall/spin.

It is quite possible to minimize risk in this area, too, because midair collisions follow a familiar pattern year after year. Most collisions, about two-thirds, occur within five miles of an airport. That is quite logical. Airplanes congregate at airports, and if most midairs occurred some-where else, it would be strange indeed.

Also logically, collisions just naturally often tend to in-volve airplanes engaged in the type of flying that occurs near airports. In a two-year collection of over 100 midair collision reports used for research material, about 70 per-cent of the airplanes were on training, pleasure, or personal flights. These types of flying account for 50 percent of the total flight hours, so some extra exposure to the midair collision hazard is clearly identified. If your flying doesn't stray far from the airport, extra effort is required to mini-mize the risk of collision.

Business and corporate flying, which is usually cross country, is responsible for about one-third of the flight hours and only about 6 percent of the aircraft involved in midair collisions. There is less exposure so there is less risk. Special purpose flying that results in airplanes congregating in one spot or flying together accounts for a number of collisions. Examples are found in fire fighting, crop control, fish spotting, hunting, and air show activities.

High Wing or Low

Another myth to dispel is that high-wing airplanes have a greater involvement in midair collisions than low-wing air-planes. In a two-year period studied, 42 percent of the powered fixed-wing airplanes in collisions were low-wing; about 45 percent of the fleet was low-wing during the pe-

riod. That leaves the high-wing birds with a little disadvantage, but the percentage of high-wing airplanes doing the
type of flying in which the midair collision hazard is highest
—training, pleasure, and personal flying—is likely greater
than the percentage of the low-wing airplanes involved in
this activity. The closeness of the high/low-wing involvement in collisions could even be interpreted as indicating
an advantage for the high wing. Perhaps the obvious visual
limitation of high-wing airplanes prompts pilots to work at
minimizing the effects of blind spots.

There is also a direct relationship between the type of
airplane and the number of collisions. Cessna 150s and
Piper PA–28s are most frequently involved. In a two-year
period, they all but tied on both the number of midairs and
the number of aircraft in the fleet. The Cessna 172 is in the
fleet in roughly similar numbers, yet its involvement in
midairs was little more than half that of the 150 and the
PA–28. That is easy to explain. Perhaps half the 172's
flying hours are in the area of high risk, while the rest are
out in the straight and level, away from airports. The
Cessna 150 and PA–28 are widely used in training and
pleasure flying. No other aircraft type had a significant
enough individual involvement in midair collisions to mention.

Density v. Collisions

A relationship between traffic density and collisions is suggested in California. California contains 12 percent of the airplanes and was the scene of 24 percent of the midair collisions in the two-year period. One might challenge the density theory with the fact that aircraft population per 1,000 square miles in California is lower than in Florida and Ohio and about the same as Illinois. However, California's airplane population is concentrated at a relatively small number of airports in metropolitan areas, and this concentration combines with mountainous terrain to greatly limit the amount of airspace that is used by light aircraft. The visibility is pretty grungy in some of the California metropolitan areas much of the time, too.

No other state shows a continuing year-to-year midair collision history that is much higher than average.

It is worthy of note that a study of seven years' worth of collisions by the MITRE Corporation might be interpreted as contradicting the California theory by showing that midair collisions at uncontrolled airports increased linearly with operations: When operations doubled, midair collisions doubled. On the just stated theory that traffic density increases hazard, it might have been more logical for collisions to triple with a doubling of operations. Perhaps, though, pilots rise to the occasion when they know they are operating at a busy uncontrolled airport, and California's problem might be more closely related to the compacting of en route VFR traffic into flyways dictated by terrain than to the state's busy airports.

Most of the general aviation operations are concentrated

at a relatively small percentage of the uncontrolled airports, with two-thirds of the operations at 8 percent of the airports. It is thus fortunate and encouraging that the collision hazard seems to increase linearly with traffic. The fact that collisions are almost directly related to operations does concentrate the action at the airports where traffic is concentrated, and this in turn might make it appear that these airports might have more than their share of collisions until the true record is examined.

At Controlled Airports

The increase in collisions with traffic is nonlinear at controlled airports. There, low-activity airports remain virtually collision-free, with the collisions increasing dramatically as VFR traffic at controlled airports increases. The increase in collisions with traffic at controlled airports underlines a basic problem. When a pilot feels there is control, he must not be as alert as when he is in a situation where it is clear that only his eyeball is protecting the tail. This must be why the operation of a tower doesn't reduce the true collision hazard. When only fatal midair collisions are considered, the rate at uncontrolled airports is not significantly higher than the rate at controlled airports. In fact, in one recent year there were more fatal midair collisions at controlled airports than at uncontrolled airports.

Configuration

As airplanes actually collide, the encounters more likely involve high wing v. high wing and high wing v. low wing airplanes. These two types of collisions accounted for over 60 percent of the total encounters. Low wing v. low wing was next, and there was what might be considered a significant number of collisions between helicopters and fixed-wing aircraft. Almost 10 percent of the midairs studied involved a helicopter and an airplane.

Helicopters?

The helicopter situation makes some suggestions. Helicopters have excellent visibility, and their involvement supports the NTSB's continuing 100 percent pilot error classification for midair collisions. The NTSB does assign other visual causal factors such as dirty windshields and sun glare to midairs, but they are generally satisfied that one and usually both pilots had the opportunity to make a timely sighting of the other traffic and maneuver to avoid the other airplane. Even when flying in a helicopter's bubble, a pilot must still make the effort to look for other aircraft.

Another thought is that helicopters move in a manner that is unpredictable to fixed-wing pilots, and this makes them hard to find and track. We have a lot of clues on where to look for fixed-wing airplanes around an airport, but where do you look for helicopters? The airplanes all use the runway, but the helicopters can use ramp areas and can come and go in any direction. And whereas it might be reasoned that helicopters are likely to tangle with fast airplanes that sneak up behind them, most helicopter collisions involve plain old light airplanes—airplanes that tend to frequent the same low-altitude airspace as the chopper.

High Performance v. Slow

I think we all consider the possibility of a high performance airplane sneaking up on a light airplane from an unlikely spot. This does happen, but not too often. In the two-year period studied, an FAA jet hit a light airplane, and two military jets hit general aviation airplanes. In the military jet accidents, it appeared that the aircraft were intercepting the slower airplane, accidentally on purpose in one case, and that has been examined and hopefully remedied by the military.

Some feel it a minor miracle that there aren't more military v. civil midair collisions because of the low-level maneuvering done by the air force on practice missions. Put into context, though, the number of missions flown divides into the size of the country to stack the odds against such encounters.

Battleground

Much has been written about the final approach at uncontrolled airports being the great midair collision battleground. This *is* an area of identifiable hazard, but there is no way to say that solving the problem on final would eliminate a substantial part of the total problem. Accidents in which both aircraft are on final at an uncontrolled airport are numerous, but they also tend to be less serious—only a small percentage were fatal in the two-year period.

These collisions at uncontrolled airports tend to occur at low altitudes; 80 percent happen below 400 feet. Also, a very high percentage involve one aircraft overtaking another, and the closure rates tend to be gradual. These two factors minimize the severity of collisions on final approach at uncontrolled airports. They also teach us when to watch out for what and offer the encouraging thought that there's usually plenty of time to find, see, and avoid the other aircraft.

More Serious

Of concern is the midair collision in which at least one airplane is moving along in a phase of flight not related to takeoff or landing. There are actually more midairs like this than there are final approach collisions, and almost 70 percent of this type of accident results in fatal injuries to the occupants of at least one airplane.

These generally occur at higher altitudes, and the collision angles and closure rates cover the spectrum. About 20 percent involve one airplane overtaking another directly from behind, but no other angle accounts for a substantial number of collisions.

The conditions of these lethal midairs follow no strict pattern, but there are some similarities. They tend to occur at relatively low cruising altitudes, with almost 90 percent occurring below 5,000 feet. In most cases, both airplanes were in normal cruising flight. In some instances, the collisions involved two training flights. Training areas are designated for flight schools, and airplanes tend to congregate in these areas so this might be expected. There is also some involvement between training flights and airplanes cruising through a training area. The areas are not identified to transient pilots, and airplanes maneuvering on training flights are following a less predictable path than an airplane flying cross-country. This makes both sighting and tracking more difficult. Also, in the training airplane there must be a tendency for both instructor and student to spend less time looking for other traffic and more time concentrating on the teaching/learning process.

In examining the individual reports, it is plain that many of the midair collisions in which one airplane is not in the traffic pattern are nevertheless closely associated with operations around an airport; that is, at least one of the aircraft was on a local flight. The record is clear in showing that the airspace near an airport is where the risk is highest, but there is enough risk elsewhere to dictate constant vigilance for other traffic.

Control Towers

The midair collisions that do occur in airport traffic areas
—that airspace below 3,000 feet within five miles of a controlled airport—tend to be unusually serious. Twelve percent of the midairs in the two-year period studied occurred
under the jurisdiction of tower control, and 85 percent of
these were fatal. During the period, there were actually
more *fatal* midair collisions under tower control than on
final approach at uncontrolled airports. And, as noted,
there isn't a significant difference in the fatal collision rate
at controlled airports and uncontrolled airports.

No Measure

While the midair collision risks can be defined and minimized just as we can do with risks in other areas, the midair
avoidance task is made difficult by the fact that there is
usually nothing tangible on which to hang the good decisions. As the work of minimizing weather risks is approached, we have large and obvious clouds to view. If
continuing VFR into marginal conditions, the outlook
changes from clarity to murkiness. If risk management is
being applied to the stall/spin, the feel of the controls, what
we see, and the airspeed indicator all start suggesting a
problem long before the critical moment. But in midair
collisions, the first inkling a pilot has of a problem is often a
life-size view of another airplane framed by the windshield

or a side window. Or it might just be the loud noise that accompanies a vigorous entanglement of airframes. The helicopter record suggests that development of a looking plan could bear a lot of fruit. The choppers have good visibility plus collisions. They prove that the deficiency is more in visual inactivity than in visual limitations.

Self-Motivation

The call is for a methodical visual collision avoidance plan based on the facts as we know them, on the visual limitations of the airplane, and on the capabilities of the eye.

Methodical in this must mean continuous. It is frightfully easy to fly along for hours on end with the gaze fixed straight ahead. If the windshield and windows of the aircraft are dirty, the eye can even tend to focus on the grime rather than the outdoors, making aircraft spotting that much more difficult. Sparkling clean windows can do a lot more for you than improve the view of the scenery; they can also make it easier, and probably more enjoyable, to keep up an active scan for other airplanes. If you wear glasses, you keep them clean. Do the same for your windows.

The plan should contain a requirement to look carefully all around the airplane. The point of focus shouldn't move continuously; rather, it is best to look, move a bit, look again, and continue around, and up, and down, with a pause every thirty degrees or so. Peripheral vision should pick up the airplanes that are not directly in the line of view. Once a comfortable scan has been developed, use it with diligence. Don't neglect the area behind the airplane, either. The closure rate of an overtaking airplane will be slower, but it will still be adequate if he gets his nose in your tail.

Keep Looking

It is more difficult to maintain interest in scanning for other traffic while en route. We seldom see other airplanes, and it is difficult to remain motivated without an occasional reward. That reasoning wouldn't diminish the severity of an en route collision, though. The most hazardous times are when flying below 5,000 feet, when passing near airports, and when operating on airways or VFR flyways, especially in congested areas. However, some hazard exists anytime more than one airplane is flying, and colliding with the only other airplane within fifty miles is just as undesirable as colliding with one of 1,000 within fifty miles.

The hazard in relation to airline jet aircraft should not be minimized. Be especially wary when within thirty miles of an airport served by air carriers. Air traffic control procedures generally promote keeping the jets above 10,000 feet until they are within thirty miles of their destination airport, and then down they come into the airspace most often used by general aviation. The lower we fly when within thirty miles of busy airline airports, the better. It

helps to listen to the automatic terminal information service, too. The jets will tend to be lower farther from the
airport in the direction from which approaches are being
conducted—on the southwest side in the case of approaches to the northeast, for example. It almost goes without saying that the areas of the ILS final approach course
should be avoided for a distance of at least ten miles from
the airport.

At the Airport

In closer to the airport, the clear call at controlled airports
is to forget that control might have some collision avoidance value when flying in VFR conditions. Base risk management entirely on seeing and avoiding other aircraft on
an individual and independent basis. The prime area of
hazard around controlled airports is in the airport traffic
area but outside the traffic pattern.

Always check crossing runways for possible conflicts before takeoff or landing, even at controlled airports. And,
for that matter, when cleared for takeoff make certain
there's not one on short final. It's sensible to take these
precautions. Collision avoidance is the pilot's responsibility
when the pilot can see, and the pilot isn't doing his or her
part unless the eye is always used to verify that what the
controller cleared you to do is indeed a good idea.

At uncontrolled airports, make use of Unicom to an-
nounce position in the traffic pattern and to monitor the

position reports of other aircraft, but still let the eyeball and the scan for other traffic reign supreme. Look for airplanes flying in the normal traffic patterns, nonstandard patterns, and straight-in approaches. Scan the unlikeliest spots for possible helicopter operations. On around closer to the runway, remember the characteristics of the classic final approach collision: One aircraft overtakes another below 400 feet and closure rates are low. Make sure that the final approach course is yours and yours alone.

There's no doubt that electronic collision avoidance devices will be developed, but the human eye will remain the best collision avoidance device in visual conditions. If airplanes are out there, the eye can find them if used properly. And there are airplanes there to be found. Soon after we were married, I appointed my bride as chief airplane spotter. To enhance interest, I offered to pay her one dollar for each airplane she spotted first. In a few weeks, I owed her a couple of hundred bucks. It was a good lesson for me. The old scan for traffic needed some burnishing.

8 | Mechanical Malaise

When starting through government publications on general aviation accidents, one fact always stares you down on an early page. It begins "Ten Most Frequent Types of Accidents," and the leader by a very wide margin is always engine failure or malfunction. If engine failure is the leading accident cause, then the single-engine airplane is suspect, right? And the answer to the problem would be an airplane with two engines, right? Not really, because the subject is far from simple. It is confused by things like the National Transportation Safety Board putting a pilot-error item such as fuel exhaustion in the engine-failure column. Regardless, as we consider the role of mechanical failures in accidents, it is common to think primarily in terms of engine failures and of the relative merits of having two engines.

130

So we'll emphasize the question of one engine v. two. This exploration is not meant to be controversial or iconoclastic; it is only to explore the record as it exists and the potential of both singles and twins.

Strike One

I had an interesting telephone conversation while gathering some figures for this subject. Everything was arranged on the desk, as if I were just waiting for the employee of a department of the U. S. government to call and say, "The people in Washington have proposed that we no longer be allowed to carry passengers in our single-engine airplanes, which we use for patrol as well as transportation. Do you have any information that would help us fight this?"

The caller was mildly surprised when I answered, "Just happen to have what you want right here. The unvarnished fact of the matter is that your chances of being completely wiped out because of an engine failure are twice as high in a twin as in a single-engine airplane. That is from a National Transportation Safety Board study, and I have independent studies in my file that corroborate this finding."

The bureaucrat thanked me for the information and went about the task of trying to convince the Washington folk that singles are okay. I don't know how he came out and wouldn't be too optimistic about his success because the prejudice against single-engine airplanes is deeply ingrained in the heads of those who embrace the theory that more is better. This is frequently seen in big business as well as big government, where edicts against employees using single-engine airplanes are common. Even when overwhelming proof is offered, many anti-single types do not waver. This could often be ego-connected. To admit that a single might fit a mission could take someone's big bird away, and nobody likes to think about that happening.

The Public

Public acceptance of light airplanes in general and single-engine airplanes in particular has long been affected by an unfounded but basic fear that the airplane will fall if the engine fails. People ask, "What do you do if the engine stops?" The newspapers almost always make some reference to engines in coverage of an accident: "The engine sputtered, and the single-engine plane crashed" or "witnesses reported that the motor of the single-engine plane was racing right before it hit."

The fact that all this might have happened as a thunderstorm raged hardly seems to matter. And the result is that many lay people believe that single-engine airplanes are inherently dangerous. The vision is of a high percentage of the brave and clean-living aviators of our land plunging power-off to the ground, despite a valiant effort to get the engine going again. The only counter is patient explanation and hope for understanding of the facts as they exist.

They Do Fail!

The first fact is perhaps the most important one. Engines do quit, both on singles and twins. But they seldom quit without provocation, and the problem usually originates in the left front seat of the airplane. We worry about connecting rods and valves, but pilot error causes more than half the engine failures. Fuel system mismanagement and fuel exhaustion are the prime causes of aerial silence. This is really pilot failure, but because the engine stops running it is also considered engine failure.

I sat flying along in my Skyhawk and thinking about this recently. I had started out from West Palm Beach, with Tallahassee listed as a destination. Tallahassee, though, was less than halfway to Little Rock, my final destination. The true plan was to go on past there to get as far as possible to insure a one-stop flight to Little Rock. Dothan, Alabama, would be halfway. How about that? No, greedy, Montgomery would be more than halfway, so keep right on going.

The fuel gauges were down in the bad part of the range before Montgomery was reached, but the one hour's fuel reserve that I consider inviolate was still in the tanks— barely. The way I rationalized this as I flew along was illustration aplenty of how one must divorce thinking from what would be nice, what would be handy, and what would be most expeditious when contemplating the amount of fuel in the tanks. A two-stop flight would have been far more desirable than a one-stop with anxiety about fuel.

Out of Fuel

How large is the fuel exhaustion problem in relation to the total engine-failure picture? In some airplanes it is huge. For example, according to an NTSB study, almost half the Cessna 172 engine-failure accidents on a five-year period were related to fuel exhaustion. On the other side of the coin, only about 12 percent of the Bonanza engine-failure accidents were caused by fuel exhaustion. That is logical because pilots flying Cessna 172s are probably more likely to become lost and waste fuel than are Bonanza pilots—if for no other reason than the more sophisticated electronics usually found in Bonanzas. A headwind accounts for a larger percentage of a 172's cruising speed and is probably a factor in fuel exhaustion accidents. Also, more Cessna 172s are in the rental airplane fleet, where pilots might not be as current as the average Bonanza pilot. And while I have no figures to back it up, a correlation could probably be drawn between a pilot's flying time in the very airplane involved and fuel exhaustion. Once you've flown an airplane for a while, you'd be less likely to use all the fuel. You know how the gauges work and you know the fuel consumption, so there might be less temptation to kid yourself. (This could be debated. Familiarity breeds contempt in some cases.)

There's yet another side to the coin, and it can also be illustrated with a 172/Bonanza comparison. Almost half the Bonanza's engine-failure accidents are related to mismanagement of fuel or trying to run the engine on a dry tank when there is still fuel in another tank. The 172, with its simpler fuel system that can be left on "both" all the time, hardly figures in fuel system mismanagement accidents. This is an item of design, as will be covered in the next chapter, but it does help outline this part of the engine-failure problem. If you are flying an airplane with a simple fuel system, your engine failure is more likely to come from running out of gas. If you are flying an airplane with a fuel system requiring management, your engine failure is more likely to come from your mismanagement of the system. In either case, a smattering of pilot diligence will cure the problem.

The Numbers

Back to the NTSB study for some numbers to contemplate. In proportionate total, singles had twice as many engine-failure accidents as twins. But four times as many twin accidents were fatal, thus the conclusion that your chances of being wiped out in a twin are twice as high as in a single. And the study actually favors twins in the sense that most twins considered were "current" airplanes, usually valuable enough for loving care and valuable enough for the insurance company to require that they be flown by pilots with some experience. The light twin didn't really come into being in quantity until the mid- to late fifties, and virtually all the twins on the list were relatively young in terms of years. The singles covered a lot more ground. Homebuilts account for a large number of engine failures, and these are all singles. Agricultural airplanes (including Stearmans) are singles, and the great fleet of airplanes built before and immediately following World War II is both old and single-engine. As an illustration of what age does to the engine-failure accident rate, it should be noted that the Cessna 140's engine-failure rate is more than twice as high as the newer 150's rate. The Cessna 170's rate is almost twice as high as the 172's rate. And some airplanes, like the old Bellancas and Navions plus the Swifts, Luscombes, and Stinsons, have comparatively astronomical engine-failure accident rates.

A Single Example

To get a better picture of the current situation, it is appropriate to take a couple of airplanes and dissect their engine-failure accident rate. The Cessna 172 is a good example of a single because it is widely used and it tends to cover the spectrum of general aviation operations. The 172s in the fleet range from business-use vehicles maintained in the finest shops, to FBO training and air-taxi aircraft, to recreational machines maintained both in good shops and under shade trees. The 172 is flown by a great variety of pilots, from student to airline transport. And despite the proclivity of pilots to use up all the fuel in 172s, the airplane has the lowest engine-failure accident rate in the single-engine fleet, as well as a lower rate than many twins.

According to numbers derived from NTSB figures, the 172 had one engine-failure accident for every 43,000 hours of operation in the five-year study period. (That does not mean there was an engine failure every 43,000 hours. It only means that for each 43,000 hours of operation, one 172 was bent badly enough after a failure for it to be considered an accident.)

Okay, now eliminate all the human error. Subtract the fuel exhaustion, starvation, and contamination; take away improper operation of the power plant controls, including things like failure to use carburetor heat or to lock the primer. Then don't count the engine-failure accidents in which poor maintenance was established as the cause of the problem. Get down to the 172 accidents following a true failure of the engine—things breaking or failing in a properly maintained engine. On this basis, the 172 was involved in one engine-failure accident for every 303,448 hours flown.

The Real Risk

Go a step further now to determine the true risk to life. The NTSB study notes that 5.4 percent of the engine-failure accidents in single-engine airplanes are fatal. So, considering only the accidents precipitated by an honest breakage of the engine, an unavoidable failure while the pilot was doing and had done everything correctly, we arrive at one engine-failure-related fatal accident for every 5,619,411 hours of Cessna 172 operation. That is one every 641.5 years if you choose to fly twenty-four hours a day. Anyone who can take that number and suggest that there is something inherently dangerous about the fact that this airplane has only one engine is beyond help. Cut it in half or divide it by ten, and there's still no suggestion of extraordinary engine-related risk when flying one of the airplanes.

Admittedly, the 172 had the best single-engine record during the period studied. The PA–28 (Cherokee) was not far behind, though. And besides increasing with age, the engine-failure accident rates also trend upward with stalling speed. Retractables tend to have a higher rate, too. The latter might come from the tendency of pilots to land retractables with the gear up in any forced landing, guaranteeing enough damage to qualify as an accident even though the landing is quite successful.

A Twin Example

For comparative purposes, the NTSB study only includes all the details on one twin that might be considered representative. This airplane does not have the best twin record, so there are apples and oranges in our comparison, but it is still worthy of consideration. The airplane is the Piper PA–23, which designation encompasses both the Apache and the Aztec. The PA–23 fleet probably averages more age and wear than the 172 fleet. Also, PA–23s are used for a wide variety of purposes and are flown by all different kinds of pilots. The airplane starts with a raw engine-failure accident rate of one for every 32,362 flying hours, as derived from NTSB figures. Eliminate all but the true mechanical failures of an engine, and the PA–23 has a failure accident every 123,263 hours. In multiengine airplanes, 22.9 percent of the engine-failure accidents are fatal, so if the PA–23's engine-failure fatal accident were to be equal to the average for the twin fleet, the airplane would appear to have a fatal accident related to the true failure of an engine every 538,264 flying hours. This is highly theoretical because, as we will see in examining stall/spin accidents by type in chapter 10, the PA–23 has a lower-than-average involvement in stall/spin accidents. So it would probably have a lower-than-average involvement in serious accidents following an engine failure because the stall/spin is usually the reason for an engine-failure accident reaching the serious stage.

Ten to One?

There are a lot of apples and oranges plus some theoretical considerations in that comparison, which shows a sample single-engine airplane coming out ten times as well as a sample twin. It perhaps proves nothing, but the numbers are from an NTSB study and I think it reasonable to go beyond the raw figures and compare engine failures as they affect pilots who live the clean life, obtain the best available maintenance for their airplanes, and don't run out of gas— to say nothing of mismanaging the fuel, letting ice accumulate in the carburetor, or doing any of the other things that pilots do to induce silence in the cabin. We can all, hope-fully, convince ourselves that an honest appraisal of risks begins (but does not end) with a look at things over which we have no control, such as a valve or a rod breaking.

Jaws

A good twin-engine pilot listened attentively to that dis-sertation on the records of a representative single v. a representative twin and then made an offer. He suggested that we go out off the shore about twenty miles, he in a twin, me in a single. Then we would each secure one engine and see what happened. He grinned like a presidential candidate, said "Jaws," and left the discussion at that. And he had a point. However, the purpose of the comparison was to show the exposure to risk that is found in the single as it is used, and I think that 5.5-million-hour figure for the 172 is encouraging.

Other Figures

To buttress the concept of the single's good record, a whole year's worth of accidents were studied individually. The ones considered were those involving engine failure with a probable cause not related to the pilot in command. The engine quit of its own accord while the pilot was operating it properly. (This sample would include engine failures caused by poor maintenance.) One reason I did this was because a person openly mentioned the Bonanza and said something like, "What about the Bonanzas that were lost last year because of engine failures?" The fact is that there was not one Bonanza involved in a fatal engine-failure accident that year that didn't list the pilot in command as the probable cause. And, as a matter of fact, no production single-engine airplane was involved in more than one such fatal accident. It is a random thing, spread very thinly and evenly throughout the fleet.

Homebuilts

It is very worthy of note, too, that in this year 35 percent of the single-engine airplanes involved in fatal engine-failure accidents where the failure was not pilot-induced were homebuilt aircraft, many of which were powered by automotive or other nonaviation-type engines. Remember that in any NTSB statistical analysis, these airplanes are considered along with the store-bought airplanes. They comprise a lot less than 35 percent of the fleet, so their record would tend to make the record of production singles look worse than it really is.

In the year studied the twins involved in the type of accident we are discussing were spread among the fleet in an even basis, too.

Agricultural Airplanes

During this year, there were no agricultural airplanes involved in fatal engine-failure accidents in which the pilot in command was not the cause. To find the dusters and sprayers, you have to go over to the nonfatal column. There are a lot there, with 20 percent of the total singles ag aircraft. This teaches a lesson that we might as well learn here as elsewhere. The agricultural airplanes participate freely in engine-failure accidents, but nobody is badly hurt. Why? Because the airplanes are designed with survivability in mind, and the pilots are wise enough to take advantage of the safety equipment. They have and use shoulder harnesses, and most wear crash helmets. If you are ever flying and tempted not to use a shoulder harness, remember the wise ag pilots; they know what is good for them.

Far on the other side of the ledger is the homebuilt: A high percentage of the engine-failure accidents in this type of airplane are fatal. They would tend to have fewer occupant protection features, so that is logical as well as illustrative.

Question

All this leads to a conclusion and a question. As airplanes are involved in fatal accidents following mechanical failures of an engine, the single comes out better. In the NTSB study, the total single-engine fleet proved to be twice as good as the total twin-engine fleet when fatal accidents following engine failure for any reason are considered. You can take the statistics and records apart, and everything makes the single look even better as things like homebuilts and agricultural aircraft are considered. The question is why. People often buy twins because they feel that they are "safer," yet the opposite seems to be the case.

When searching through the NTSB study for answers, it is obvious that twins have a lot of things in common with singles. About 50 percent of the fatal engine-failure accidents happen within a mile of an airport, twin or single. Approximately the same percentage of the serious engine-failure accidents are during dual instruction, twin or single. And the engine-failure accident in the initial climb phase of flight accounts for 28 percent of the airplanes destroyed in both categories, twin and singles.

These areas of similarity are noteworthy because they show that while there might be a striking theoretical difference between singles and twins, John Q. Pilot finds the bite remarkably alike when things are done incorrectly.

With half the fatal accidents close to the airport and 28 percent of the aircraft wiped out after a failure during initial climb, we can speculate that the pilot of a twin is incapable of cashing in on any advantage that his airplane has over a single. The return-and-land after a failure apparently presents an equally difficult task to the pilot of either class airplane. Further, a failure anywhere in the pattern or a landing back on the runway with an engine out, whether it be *the* engine in a single or *one* engine in a twin, appears to present a problem of the same magnitude to the pilot, twin or single.

Instructional Flying

The roughly equal percentage of singles and twins involved in engine-failure-related fatal accidents while engaged in instructional flying shows that any asymmetrical thrust problems in twins during low-speed training operations did not unduly affect the record during the one-year period covered by my study.

Reasons

But when contemplating each class of airplane, the apparent differences in concept make it obvious that while they might have the same problems after the engine fails, they must have the problems for different reasons. And there must be reasons for more serious consequences in twins.

Simplicity is one basic thing in favor of a single. The 172 probably has the best single-engine record because there is little to malfunction and because the power plants used in that airplane since its introduction are legendary for their reliability. (As 80-octane fuel disappears, this reliability might suffer, as there are numerous problems related to using 100-octane fuel in these engines.) Low landing speed is another advantage. If a single is flown into anything other than a brick wall or the dead center of a tree, and if the arrival is at a gentle angle and a speed not far above stall, chances are the people will fare tolerably well. Shoulder harnesses make this even better, as proven by the agricultural airplanes. The harnesses are very effective in the low-speed, low-angle accidents that can characterize even the most tedious forced landings, provided reasonable pilot technique prevails.

Apparently against the single is the fact that it does indeed have but one engine. If that one fails, there is no alternative to a landing in the very near future. However, it is possible to be optimistic and consider this an advantage, rather than a disadvantage, for at least some pilots. In the single the inevitability of the forced landing might help the pilot's mental processes. There is no doubt about what is going to happen, so do your best. In the twin there can appear to be more alternatives. To protect one's image, a twin should always be landed on an airport, right? It is probably difficult for some pilots to accept any failure of this concept, whether its elusiveness becomes obvious in initial climb or as the airplane goes low on an approach slope. The twin pilot is faced with more temptations and challenges to judgment after an engine failure, and the demand is for a top-notch professional job of planning and flying for the length of time it takes to reach an airport and land.

Stall/Spin

In either class of airplane, the failing grade on an engine-out landing most often comes when the pilot stalls the airplane. The stall/spin is the leading killer in both. And the stall/spin is where the single gains its advantage over the twin. According to NTSB numbers, 24.6 percent of the twin accidents following engine failure were of the type, usually stall/spin, that produce fatal or serious injuries. By contrast, 7.5 percent of the single-engine accidents were of this serious nature.

Double Trouble

The reason the twin has a relatively higher involvement in stall/spin accidents has to be related to both the nature of the machine and to human nature. The desire is to keep on flying even though half the power is gone. All the light twins have limited performance with an engine out. If the pilot fails to recognize a situation in which the airplane is not capable of climbing over obstacles, for example, and tries to make it climb over them anyway, a stall/spin is the likely result. The configuration of all the airplanes (except the Cessna Skymaster) has a lot to do with the question, too. When the engines are on the wings and when the power is halved, the remaining half is all on one side. The thrust is not symmetrical, and if the pilot lets the airspeed decay, this can cause directional control to start deteriorating. When this begins to become obvious, the pilot who is unwilling to lower the nose of the aircraft and reduce thrust as necessary to restore directional control is only seconds away from trouble. And it isn't easy to lower the nose and reduce power on the operative engine when the trees are tickling your feet.

Finally, the twin's stalling speed is likely higher than that of a single, so any off-airport landing is at a higher speed. As far as survivability goes, the prime things that count are the speed at impact and the distance it takes to stop. I've seen a single-engine airplane go through the window of an automobile showroom without great damage to the pilot. I've seen one go through the roof of a building, and I've seen them left in the tops of trees without great damage to the occupants. Twins are bigger, heavier, and harder to deposit in such impromptu surroundings without mussing your hair. And when you use all the fuel in a twin or mismanage the fuel system, the airplane is likely to require a completely impromptu arrival. Twin pilots don't make fuel mistakes nearly as often as single pilots, but it does happen.

Theory

In theory the twin should have less involvement in engine-failure-related accidents, and the theory holds water in non-fatal accidents. But it is just not realized when serious accidents are considered. Some engine-out related accidents illustrate this.

During a dual training flight the instructor-pilot was obviously giving the student some minimum control speed drill when the airplane stalled and entered a spin. There was not adequate altitude for recovery.

A pilot flying a twin that was loaded to well over gross weight had an engine failure in initial climb. The prop on the offending engine was not feathered, but the airplane

probably wouldn't have climbed anyway because of its
overweight condition. There are many times when a twin
should be flown well below gross weight to maintain single-
engine climb capability in high density altitude conditions.

For another, the pilot positioned one engine's fuel selector to a dry tank. That engine failed, and the pilot subsequently let the airspeed decay. The final result was a stall/
spin.

A scenario that constantly recurs finds a pilot losing
control of a twin on an engine-out approach. In these cases,
the engine usually fails en route, giving the pilot plenty of
time to plan the approach. But for some reason, a proper
approach slope is not maintained. The problem is usually
related to premature extension of the landing gear and
flaps, going low on the approach slope, and letting the airspeed decay in the attempt to correct. Once those things
have been blended into the situation, most twins are incapable of making it to the runway. And the pilot loses
control of the airplane in the process of trying to make it do
the impossible. It is a simple matter of poor flying technique. The ending is similar to that found when a pilot of a
single-engine airplane might stall and spin trying to reach a
field beyond the gliding capability of the airplane during a
forced landing.

Good Operating Practices

The similarity of the problems encountered by single and twin pilots after an engine failure suggests that simple good operating practices to minimize the risks of engine failure might also be similar.

The time from lift-off to, say, 1,000 feet above the ground might be considered a time of maximum vulnerability to engine failure in any airplane. Once at 1,000 feet, there is enough energy stored, primarily in the form of altitude, to enjoy some options if the engine of a single fails or a few more options if one engine on a twin fails. The clear call is for a full-power climb at the airplane's best rate-of-climb speed to 1,000 feet above the surface on *every* takeoff. That maximizes performance and minimizes vulnerability.

Using full power for initial climb is very important. Figures at the FAA Aeronautical Center indicate that 80.7 percent of the actual mechanical failures of engines occurred during a power change. That is a good enough reason not to reduce power in the early stages of an initial climb. If the engine spins up properly at the start of the takeoff run, just leave the little darling spinning until some altitude is in the bank, in a single or a twin. Most general aviation engines are approved for continuous full-power operation, and those that have limitations are approved for full-power long enough to reach 1,000 feet under most any conditions. In situations where more than 1,000 feet appears to be advantageous before contemplating the risks involved in a power loss, just keep on climbing wide open at the best rate-of-climb speed until at a higher altitude.

There's simply no more efficient way to get the most altitude in the least time.

A twin pilot should be current and proficient in the
transition from the twin-engine best rate-of-climb speed at
full power to the single-engine best rate-of-climb speed
after an engine failure. This transition must be made without allowing the airspeed to decay below the best single-
engine climb speed.

Arrivals

On the other end of the line, vulnerability to serious accident during an engine-out arrival can be minimized by
knowing how to put the airplane on a selected spot after an
engine failure. In a single this becomes the power-off spot
landing, ending in a touchdown at the selected location at
minimum speed. In a twin it's a single-engine approach to a
runway down a slope that requires about 40 percent power
on the operating engine with the gear and approach flaps
down. On that basis, there is some power to reduce if the
approach is trending on the high side and more power to
add if it is trending toward the low side. If it gets danger-
ously low, the gear could be retracted to cut drag. Twin or
single, the simple fact that the point on the ground toward
which the airplane is going remains constant in the windshield is a key to judging and managing the approach.

To Sum Up

The twin v. single involvement in total engine-failure accidents is logical. The single does have twice as many total engine-failure-related accidents because the possibility of landing in a random area is quite high after the engine fails on a single, and some damage is likely to result from such a landing even if it offers no real hazard to the occupants of the airplane. The twin's *fatal* accident rate following engine failure is twice as high as the single's because the consequences of a mistake in a twin prove to be numerically four times greater than in a single.

The total of the single v. twin question is positive, too. The single's excellent record is a direct result of mechanical reliability, simplicity, and low stalling speed. The twin's record could be even better than the single, and would be if the human element were not so strongly against the virtues of the multiengine airplane. The pilots flying twins must only recognize the requirement for an extremely high level of proficiency combined with a complete understanding of the airplane's capability to take most of the engine-failure risk out of the twin picture.

In Addition

There's another area where mechanical failure is a question and the twin has a good answer. There are a few accidents in which the failure of a vacuum or electrical system in a

single-engine airplane becomes the straw that breaks the
pilot's back. These systems are redundant in almost all
twins, and the consequences of failure of half the vacuum
or electric power are very minor. All the single-engine pilot
can do is equip with warning systems to give timely word of
a failure and learn to operate the airplane properly with
one of the systems inoperative.

Propeller Problems

There are not a lot of other mechanical things that break
and cause serious problems. Propellers do occasionally fail,
with disastrous results in a few instances. If a whole blade
goes, the imbalance can cause the engine to leave the airplane, but this is rare indeed. Or a blade can do damage to
some part of the airframe. Props are like anything else,
though, and respond favorably to tender loving care and
unfavorably to neglect. Good maintenance is the key to
avoiding propeller problems.

Big Single

One other check mark must be put on the twin's side of the
ledger before leaving the subject of the relationship between mechanical reliability, the number of engines, and

accidents. From a practical standpoint many twin-engine airplanes have two engines because they need two engines. An airplane of their total horsepower, speed, and capacity simply would not be practical with one engine. The redundancy of systems is deemed necessary, and the weight of the aircraft and the wing loading are just not such that you would want to accept the absolute risk of a random landing if the only engine should quit. Once an airplane reaches a certain size, there is no question that two engines might be required. Below that size, the argument will rage on for years. And if twin pilots will get their act straight, they might someday make the record more logical than it is today.

9 | Miscellaneous Hazards

Most all of the serious accidents fall in one of the categories covered, but there are a few hazardous items leftover. These do not account for a substantial number of annual problems, but that doesn't soften their hostile nature.

With a Busted Something

The NTSB's computer calls one troublemaker "attempted operation with known deficiencies in equipment." That would cover a multitude of mechanical sins uncovered dur-

154

ing preflight or maintenance and not repaired before flight. Or it might relate to a failure of something remedied by an airworthiness directive that had been overlooked by the pilot or shop servicing the aircraft.

Airframes are sturdy and trustworthy items, and it's rare indeed to find an accident that is related to some honest failure of the bird. When something *does* break, it is usually after the pilot overloads the structure during maneuvers or after a loss of control.

Poor maintenance causes a few problems, but serious accidents caused by the pilot blasting off with a known deficiency outnumber those caused by an honest failure of airframe parts 2:1. And in many of the honest failure cases, operation with a known deficiency could have been a companion cause. If a pilot goes off with a known loose widget and that widget fails, the cause would fall in both categories.

Propellers

There are a number of accidents involving people v. propellers. As noted in chapter 3, many of these occur at night. In most cases, the person hit by the propeller is not a pilot. Some bystanders and ground personnel walk into props, but most participants seem to be passengers.

A passenger might disembark to go do something for the pilot, such as turn on hangar lights or make arrangements for aircraft parking, and walk into the propeller. Perhaps the passenger is just entering or leaving the aircraft when the engine is running and goes in the wrong direction. I think all pilots have had passengers say, "Oh, don't shut it down; I'll just hop out." That is bad news. The only safe way is not to allow anyone to enter or leave the airplane with the engine running. On a twin some feel it is okay to let people enter and leave with the engine on the door side secured and the other one running, as the airlines often do, but remember that the airlines have ground personnel watching the passengers to make sure nobody gets over on the wrong side of the airplane.

Starting

Some people v. propeller accidents are related to hand propping. Propping is a lost art, and it seems unwise to let anyone who is not experienced attempt a hand start.

There is a related accident where the scenario calls for the pilot to prop the airplane without anyone at the controls and for the airplane to go do its own thing, wreaking havoc on the way. In one such accident, the pilot left a nonpilot inside, the engine started, and the airplane took off with its passenger and flew around for some time before crashing.

It is clearly unwise to prop an airplane without a pilot seated at the controls. There might be one exception: We used to prop J–3 Cubs from behind with one hand near the throttle and one hand on the prop, and I can't recall anyone having trouble with that procedure. But I do remember one lad, an accomplished J–3 pilot, trying to do the same trick on a Champion one morning and letting a perfectly good airplane impale itself in the side of the hangar.

Controller's Errors

There are a few fatal accidents every year in which an air traffic controller was deemed to have made an error. Controllers are human, and while they generally do their job with more uniformity than pilots, it's important to keep tabs on them and watch for a mistake. It is healthy to keep track of position when being vectored, especially when there is high terrain around or when there are obstructions near an airport. Someone telling you which way to point the airplane and the altitude at which you are expected to fly isn't a signal for the pilot to become a thoughtless robot.

The responsibility for the safe conduct of a flight belongs entirely to the pilot in command. It is a mistake to feel that any responsibility can be transferred to the ground or that controllers can affect a recovery from a precarious situation created by the pilot. People on the ground can aid a pilot by furnishing information; the pilot must interpret the information, apply it to the flight, and make the decisions.

Vortex Turbulence

Vortex turbulence from heavy aircraft can be very upsetting to smaller aircraft, and a few years ago it appeared that this might become a major safety problem. Airports with a high concentration of both air carrier jets and light airplanes were ripe for wake turbulence accidents, and a number of them occurred. The FAA did good work, though, with research into the nature of wake turbulence, with educational programs, and with air traffic control procedures designed to preclude wake turbulence encounters. In one recent year, there was only one serious wake turbulence accident, and it had a bit of freakish nature. The pilot departed behind a jet airliner, and everything would have been okay had the pilot not aborted the takeoff because of a rough engine. If the climb had continued, the flight path would have been above the jet's wake; on the abort, the pilot descended into the wake turbulence and lost control of the aircraft.

The principles of wake turbulence are relatively simple. The wing tip vortices settle, so always maintaining a flight path above the path flown by a preceding heavier airplane will keep the vortex safely below. If flight must be conducted below a heavy aircraft, the rule is to fly at least 1,000 feet below. The vortices tend to start degenerating some by the time they have settled 1,000 feet. Whenever in doubt, add some extra time or altitude.

Simple Mistake

There is one basic, recurring error that is always perplexing: Every year a few pilots attempt a takeoff with the control locks installed. The results are quite predictable. This even happens in airplanes with internal control locks —devices that are in the full view of the pilot before the takeoff is attempted. A person would have to ignore completely the "controls free" part of a checklist to fall victim to control locks.

More Minor Items

In moving away from serious accidents, it is best not to dismiss things that don't hurt as meaningless. Every fender bender counts. It has been said that even after a minor accident, a pilot must fly for 500 hours without incident lest he be classified as "accident-prone." Circumstances would have to be considered in any such classification, but there is no doubt that all accident types should be studied and avoided. The most minor accident can be a sign of weakness in technique or judgment and an indication of bigger and worse things to come. There's also a quality of "total awareness" that enables safe pilots to land on their feet every time. A minor accident reflects a flaw in this awareness.

As might be expected, a high percentage of the relatively minor mishaps are landing accidents. These often happen in high wind conditions, as covered in chapter 4, but there's one more thing to offer on this subject.

The Ercoupe, general aviation's first tricycle-gear airplane built in quantity, had its share of landing accidents as it moved into the fleet in force right after World War II. The Ercoupe's problems were precisely the same ones that lead to many landing accidents today, and the Ercoupe sales organization outlined it quite well in a 1948 newsletter, from which the following excerpts are made:

> no difficulties with landing should be encountered if a few simple and easy rules are taught and observed. . . . The most prevalent error in landing the Ercoupe is *too much airspeed on final approach*. . . . It further appears that some pilots are under the impression that the Ercoupe nose gear should be used like a battering ram. . . . The Ercoupe should be landed in a nose-up attitude. . . . Excellent results can be obtained from a full-stall landing. . . . Don't land nosewheel first; it won't work for long. . . . Don't shove the wheel forward.

Sympathy for the Ercoupe salesman's dilemma is easy to find. As tricycles became the standard, other airplane builders watched as pilots developed the same bad habits that plagued the Ercoupe thirty years ago. Despite the tricycle gear, 30 percent of the total accidents occur during the level-off, touchdown, or rollout phase of flight.

Speedy

The first thing mentioned in the Ercoupe newsletter, excessive airspeed on final, is still a primary cause of landing accidents. Pilots *know* that the stall/spin is a leading accident type, and flying with a little extra airspeed margin above the stall can seem prudent even when there's no wind-induced turbulence to harass the pilot. Too much of a good thing turns to bad, though, and excessive airspeed can only lead to bad landings regardless of wind.

Landing characteristics are tailored to an approach speed 30 percent above the stall. There is certainly enough margin in this. Approach a bit slower, and the airplane is still manageable through the flare and to touchdown. Carry a bit of extra speed because of turbulence and wind gusts, and the landing can still be graceful. Go too far either side of that normal approach speed, though, and the situation will deteriorate. Too slow, and you wind up in the stall/spin chapter; too fast, and there might be a relatively minor accident or things could progress into a major event if a go-around is attempted late or if the airplane goes into rough stuff off the end of the runway at high speed.

The Message

The tricycle expects to be landed on the rear wheels first and to have the little nosewheel lowered to the runway rather gently. Most landing accidents occur when pilots do it backward and land on the nosewheel first.

We purists have long tried to sell the full-stall landing as a solution to the problem, but it is as hard to sell in tricycles today as it was thirty years ago, when the Ercoupe was exploring the world of the general aviation pilot v. the nosewheel. Many pilots are just not going to work at a full-stall landing unless they absolutely have to. And there is a viable alternative, called the *attitude landing* by some. If those who reject the full-stall landing would only at least accept the attitude landing theory, the majority of the landing accidents would cease. Either way works.

All you must do is pick an attitude for touchdown that results in the main wheels touching first. The airplane isn't allowed to touch until it is in that attitude, which insures that the nosewheel isn't involved in the initial ground contact.

The annual cost of landing accidents is high, and it's too bad. The tricycle landing gear offers a lot of advantages, but the rules of landing really remain much the same as in the old taildraggers.

Oh, I Forgot

In some of those landing accidents, the pilot's approach and touchdown technique might be perfect, but an error of omission might cause the whole thing to end as an embarrassing disaster. Forgetting to extend the gear on a retractable or retracting it after landing is rather common. There's an old saying about this: "There are pilots who have done it, and there are pilots who are going to do it." It's not that bad, but everyone flying a retractable should be alert to the possibility. I use the mental prelanding GUMP drill (gas, undercarriage, mixture, and prop) on every arrival, whether or not the airplane is a retractable. After landing, I also find it best not to retract the flaps, fiddle with the cowl flaps, or attend to anything other than directional control and stopping until clear of the runway. Gear and flap switches are in different positions in different airplanes, and not moving anything until there is time to study the situation should help avoid retracting the gear instead of the flaps in the landing roll. Most airplanes do have switches to preclude gear retractions when on the ground, but these switches often don't function when there's not a lot of weight on the wheels, as is the case early in the landing roll.

The circumstances surrounding gear-up landings are often unusual, with the pilot distracted from the normal routine. One standard gear-up theme is a landing following a go-around. The gear and flaps are extended for the first approach, and on the go-around the gear is retracted and the flaps brought to a climb setting. The go-around pattern is flown at a rather low altitude. Flaps are extended on base or final for the second try, and quite a lot of power is used to fly the airplane to the runway. The first bad news the pilot gets is when the throttle is chopped to land. The gear horn blows at about the same time the tender belly starts scraping the runway and the prop blades begin flailing the surface.

Once the mistake is made, and the airplane has contacted the runway, it can be very dangerous to try to salvage the situation. There have been instances where a pilot has heard the prop tips hitting the runway and has managed to pull up, extend the gear, and land safely. But there have also been instances of the pilot attempting a go-around after the prop has suffered too much damage, resulting in an accident much more serious than a simple belly slide.

There are other variations on the theme, but that covers most of them. Just remember that even the most minor accident is serious in the sense that it might reflect a basic weakness that will lead to more serious things in the future.

10 | Problems Peculiar to Class and Type

Airplane salesmen often make the mistake of using safety as a sales tool. One ploy is to point out some allegedly fatal flaw in a competitor's airplane in an attempt to scare a prospect away from it and into the cockpit of the airplane that just happens to be in the hangar and available for immediate delivery. Another is to use an actual accident: "You remember old Joe, rest his soul? If he had just been flying one of *my* airplanes, he'd have made it." Such tactics are unwise because it is possible to take accident statistics and use them to crucify *any* airplane. The truth is that, given similar uses and equal exposures, the accident rates of all contemporary airplanes are fairly close to each other. When there are differences, there are usually logical reasons.

165

None of this means that design has no effect on safety. It does, but not usually in a clandestine manner. Airplanes don't do well at keeping secrets. For example, the Cessna 150 has a simple on-off fuel system, whereas the Piper Cherokee has a left-right system that requires management. The 150 has virtually no involvement in fuel system mismanagement accidents; the Cherokees have frequent involvement in that type of mishap. The 150 is clearly a more spirited airplane at the stall than a Cherokee and is a much easier airplane to spin. The Cherokee has a below average involvement in stall/spin accidents; the 150's involvement is above average. All factors must balance each other, though, because the two airplanes wind up with about the same accident rate. But if the strong points of both airplanes were shared, who could argue that they might not both enjoy a lower accident rate?

The individual pilot's cue is to learn enough about each airplane flown to avoid the things that cause trouble. I suppose an argument could be made for absolute standardization in all airplanes, with all equal in every area, but that would stifle individualism in design. Besides, who would ever agree on what's right and what's wrong? In the case of the 150 v. the Cherokee, for example, you can get quite an argument going about the stall characteristics of the two airplanes. Some instructors hold that the Cherokee is so docile at the stall that you can't really teach a student much about stalls in one of the airplanes. Others hold that the Cherokee fuel system is really better than the 150's because the pilot can manage fuel better by selecting between tanks on long trips. These arguments will never be settled.

Stall/Spin v. Type

The stall/spin phenomenon is a good place to start on accidents by make and model because it involves basic aerodynamics and flying technique.

A National Transportation Safety Board study on stall/spin accidents rated aircraft by stall/spin accident frequency. In noncommercial pleasure, practice, and business flying the following aircraft rated "very high" in relation to the average stall/spin accident frequency for all aircraft: Aeronca 11 series, Aeronca 7 series, Cessna 150 series, Cessna 177 series, Luscombe 8 series, Piper J–3/PA–11 series, Piper PA–18 series, and Taylorcraft B series.

All the aircraft in the "very high" grouping, save one, have something in common. They were designed to be easy to spin. Most are of pre- or immediately post-World War II vintage, when spins were a required maneuver. These airplanes are now flown in the recreational flying fleet where the temptation to engage in high-risk types of flying, such as buzzing or low circling, is greatest. Also, the engines in the older airplanes are not as reliable as newer engines, leading to more forced landings—a high-stall/spin-risk area. The maintenance probably leaves something to be desired in many, too. And pilots of the older airplanes probably don't fly many hours a year and thus aren't able to maintain a high level of proficiency.

The 150 and 177

All that is very logical, but what about the Cessna 150 and the Cessna 177 (Cardinal)? As noted, the 150 by design is also an easy airplane to spin. In fact, it is probably one of the best training airplanes built for spin demonstrations. The airplane spins beautifully, and the fact that it does so just naturally means there will be more accidental spins. The 150 is also in the recreational flying fleet in good numbers. After flight schools use them for a few years, they usually move on to private owners who use the airplanes for recreational flying in the same manner they use Luscombes, Aeroncas, and the like.

One other factor might also bear on the 150's stall/spin accident frequency. The airplane's static longitudinal stability is not strong—meaning that it does not take much push or pull effort on the control wheel to move the elevators and accomplish a change in pitch attitude. This is especially true when the flaps are extended. Most pilots like the 150's light elevators, and instructors often say it is the best available teaching tool because of them. The response to control inputs is brisk, and a student clearly sees the result of anything he or she does. The airplane has a pure feel to it, unencumbered by artificial devices, such as downsprings to buttress longitudinal stability. But you do have to pull back on the wheel to move an airplane from a normal angle of attack to a stalled angle of attack, and there is bound to be at least a slight correlation between stick forces required to stall and the frequency of stall/spin involvement in accidents. When greater force is required to fly the airplane at an angle of attack higher than that for which the airplane is trimmed, the message about "too slow" is just that much clearer. Be aware that the message might not be so strong in this airplane, and you can have the best of both worlds in a 150—an airplane with light, responsive elevators plus low risk in the stall/spin area.

The Cessna 177's (Cardinal) "very high" involvement is a little puzzling because the airplane is not generally used for the type of flying that leads to stall/spin problems. There were not many Cardinals in the fleet when the study was made, though, so the sample could have really been too small to be meaningful. Also, at the time, all the 177s in the fleet were the original 150-hp versions of the airplane. These were later modified in the field to improve handling qualities.

Low Involvement

Single-engine airplanes listed in the NTSB study as having "low" involvement in stall/spin accidents were the Cessna 172 series, Cessna 180 series, Cessna 206 series, and the Piper PA–24 series. "Very low" involvement was found with the Bonanzas, Cessna 182 series, Cessna 210 series, and Piper PA–28 series.

Even though the NTSB study grouped all the airplanes mentioned so far as used for noncommercial pleasure, practice, and business flying, the uses are really dissimilar. This is illustrated by which airplanes are on which list. The bulk in the "very high" category were two-place airplanes, used for local flying. The "low" and "very low" airplanes are types more likely used for transportation; the exposure to risk is thus lower. The role exposure to risk plays is perhaps most clearly illustrated by the fact that the Cessna 150 is "very high" and the Cessna 172 is "very low." Even though the 172s that were in the fleet when the study was made had stall/spin characteristics very similar to the 150, the airplane came out a lot better. Why? Because pilots didn't try to do with the 172 what they did with the 150 on the way to trouble.

Retractables

The retractables—the Bonanza, 210, and Comanche—are all airplanes with brisk stall characteristics. An inadvertent low-level stall, especially in a turn, would likely turn into disaster in any of them. But pilots of these airplanes tend to be more experienced, with more awareness of the serious nature of a stall. They seldom go buzzing, too.

Contemplating the PA–28 series, the Cherokees, is made difficult by the fact that all the four-place Cherokees, from the trainer to the retractable Arrow, are PA–28s. Some of the airplanes are engaged in training and local flying, and others are used like Bonanzas and 210s. The basic design's very low involvement in the stall/spin type of accident is a strong argument for airplanes that are difficult to spin, though.

Twins

Among twin-engine airplanes, the departures from normal in the NTSB study are the Beech Travel Air and Baron models with a relatively high involvement in stall/spin accidents, the Piper PA–23 (Apache and Aztec) with a low involvement, and the Piper Twin Comanche with a very high involvement.

The type of flying given for the Travel Air and Baron is noncommercial pleasure, practice, and business. It is difficult to see why this airplane has a higher than average stall/spin accident history when engaged in this type of operation, and from studying some other tables I think I see a possible reason for the classification. The NTSB's information shows these airplanes with a very low involvement in instructional flying, yet the airplanes are quite widely used in instructional flying. I suspect that some training accidents wound up in the wrong column, and that if the Travel Air/Baron does have a much higher than average stall/spin involvement, it is related to training and demonstration flying, not to transportation flying.

The Apache and Aztec's low involvement, even in training, is directly related to the very tame stall characteristics and good engine-out handling qualities of the airplanes. The Twin Comanche had problems during the time period covered by the report for this discussion because it was in wide use for multiengine training and because the airplane does have a tendency to spin if mishandled at the stall and to be difficult in spin recovery if all power is not retarded as the airplane enters the spin. Its history is a good illustration of how a type of airplane can develop an unfortunate record.

The FAA

Some years ago, before and during the period covered by the NTSB report, accidents in multiengine training were much more common than they are today. Part of the blame for this could be attributed to the FAA. In an attempt to make sure that every multiengine pilot had seen it all, the FAA formerly all but required demonstrations of minimum single-engine control speed (Vmc) at low altitudes. An old FAA advisory circular went through the effort of describing the "sudden power spin" that might develop if Vmc and the stall are reached at the same time and then went on to say: "Start the demonstration at such an altitude that the engine-out minimum control speed is not attained below 500 feet above the ground." The implication was that they wanted it done at low altitude, and some of the inspectors required it. At one point, you could even draw correlation between the twin training accidents and the individual requirements of the FAA offices involved. One office I knew of required Vmc demonstrations at 500 feet and had a number of training accidents in its district. In another, the supervising inspector disagreed with this method of training and testing, and there were no such accidents in his district.

Why did FAA imply that such an obviously dangerous maneuver should be attempted? The reason is logical. The posted Vmc is based on full power, and without turbocharging, full power is available only at sea level in standard conditions. When flying a normally aspirated twin at altitude, Vmc moves below the stall. So do it as low as possible to keep Vmc above the stall. The trouble was with Vmc being close to the stall even at low altitude. On the

Twin Comanche, for example, posted Vmc was originally seventy knots. (It was later raised because of this problem.) Stall speed is sixty-five knots, so a literal interpretation of the FAA's advisory circular of the time led instructors to have students fly within five knots of the stall at altitudes as low as 500 feet. The results were predictable, and even FAA inspectors were not immune to this type of accident. For a while there were so many accidents that it seemed the FAA was licensing the survivors of their prescribed multiengine curriculum.

Single-Engine Stalls?

It was also possible that back in the good old days some instructors were having students intentionally do stalls in airplanes like the Twin Comanche with one engine throttled and the other running. The FAA has always denied having condoned this, but in an advisory circular that remained in effect from 1963 to 1966, the word was: "The applicant will be required to perform stalls with engine throttled on small multiengine airplanes in both landing and cruise configurations." Note that "engine" was singular. If it was a misprint, why did the FAA not correct it in three years?

Anyway, all that has changed now, and the FAA has finally come to realize, after considerable prodding with facts, that exploring the seamy side of stalls in light twins and fooling around with Vmc demonstrations at low altitude are both lethal practices. And the accident record is a lot better than it used to be. There are still some stall/spin accidents in multiengine training, to be sure, but they must occur simply because someone didn't get the word about not provoking the airplanes at low altitudes.

One final and interesting observation on the multiengine training problem came from two different pilots engaged in checkout and instructional flying in the Twin Comanche during a period when that airplane was having an inordinate amount of accidents. One, now an FAA inspector, told me that he had done more spins in the Twin Comanche than he could count. His rosy cheeks were evidence of the fact the airplane will recover from a spin. He noted that closing the throttles as the airplane started into the spin and instituting immediate standard recovery methods would catch it every time. This pilot and another experienced Twin Comanche instructor both noted that as pilots rode the Twin Comanche into a spin, they almost always had full aileron applied against the direction of roll in an effort to stop the spin. That aggravates instead of helping, and both remarked that pilots never seemed to use rudder in an effort to arrest yaw at the stall.

Too Late

In the case of the Twin Comanche, understanding of the airplane's problem came too late. It developed a reputation, and sales sagged. Then the airplane was dropped. It is

frisky at the stall, but it is also very economical transportation. It will actually fly for about the same money as a
250-hp single Comanche.

It must be stressed that mention of airplanes having high
or low involvement in stall/spin accidents does not reflect
on an airplane's overall accident rate or history. It is just
one area, and where an airplane might tend to have more
trouble there, its nature might protect it elsewhere and
make it come out about even.

Example: Ercoupe

It's good to reflect on one very noble effort at completely
taming the stall/spin characteristics of the general aviation
airplane. The Ercoupe, produced in quantity in 1946 and
1947, would not spin, and the stall, such as it was, was
more of a high sink rate than anything else. This was in the
day when the stall/spin led the list of serious accident
causes, and in addressing this problem the Ercoupe should
have had a magnificent safety record. It did not, though.
The Ercoupe had by far the worst fatal accident rate in the
fleet, according to a study published in *Air Facts* magazine
in 1954.

Certainly the Ercoupe's good stall/spin characteristics
didn't put it at the bottom of the pile on safety. And in
reflecting on the Ercoupe's problem, its record must be related to the pilot. It was offered as a simple airplane; pilots
were licensed in Ercoupes in less time than other aircraft,

and people must have flown the airplane with a feeling that it was completely tame. As a result, the Ercoupe was piled up for reasons other than stall/spin—at an astounding rate. It is a clear example that the key to safety in airplanes is the pilot. The designer can make the airplane mannerly, but only the pilot can fly it safely.

Weather v. Type

Weather accidents are rather predictable. In an informal study of a three-year supply of these, the airplanes most used for cross-country flying were found to have the highest involvement, as would be expected. Bonanzas, Barons, 210s, 310s, Comanches, Aztecs, and the like all figured more prominently in weather accidents than did airplanes like the Cessna 150.

When you say "weather accident," some wave a red flag with "doctor and Bonanza" on it. An alleged fatal triangle that involves physicians, Bonanzas, and weather has become almost legendary.

How does the Bonanza come out in actual practice? When computed on the basis of the number of weather accidents per 100,000 hours flown, the Bonanza comes out at about the average point when compared with airplanes used in a similar manner. It would probably be a shade better than average if compared on a per-mile basis. The Bonanza's weather accident rate is, for example, 40 percent higher than the Cessna 172's on an hourly basis. But the

Bonanza's maximum cruising speed is also greater than the 172's—more than 40 percent greater when current models are compared.

In total, studying weather accidents by type does not offer many variations. If you find one airplane above average in one year, it might be below average in the next year. The VFR v. IFR involvement by type is totally predictable, too. The Cessna 172, for example, was involved only in weather accidents related to attempted VFR flight in adverse weather conditions during quite a long period of time. The 172 fleet just doesn't fly a lot of IFR hours, so low exposure is the reason for that. Likewise, the Bonanza and the light twins tend to be involved in a greater proportionate number of weather accidents during IFR flight operations than other types simply because they fly more IFR.

Airframe Failures

Airframe failures in flight in weather-related accidents are worth examining separately by type if only to keep the record straight.

This phenomenon almost always occurs in airplanes with retractable landing gear. In a three-year period, no less than 90 percent of the airplanes involved in airframe-failure accidents were retractables.

This does not suggest that retractables are harder for a person to fly in clouds or turbulence. Nor are they "weaker" in any sense. The airplanes are simply clean aerodynamically, and once a pilot lets a retractable go its own way, the airspeed buildup is likely to be rapid. The red line, the never-exceed speed, is quickly exceeded. It is for this reason that retractables are more prone to airframe failures than fixed-gear airplanes.

Spiral Dive

When retractables or any other airplanes fail in flight, it is often related to a spiral dive. Such a thing comes to most airplanes naturally: Almost all will finally wind off into a spiral dive if you leave them alone. And when there's a problem in weather, the airplane's natural tendency to spiral is probably aided and abetted by the pilot. For example, a hasty turn after entering weather might upset the pilot's orientation and make him try to fly by the seat of the pants when only the instruments tell the tale. Certainly when a pilot inadvertently penetrates weather and decides to turn, there would be some desire to turn around as quickly as possible. This can lead to overbanking.

When an airplane settles into a spiral, which is a stable situation—an equilibrium where the forces trying to steepen the spiral are finally equalized by the forces trying to make the airplane return to level—the angle of bank will be steep (probably about sixty degrees) and the nose-down pitch attitude might be as much as twenty-five degrees. The airspeed will be much higher than the speed the airplane had been flying at in level flight. Airplanes don't often fail in the spiral itself though, because it is a stable maneuver with constant pressures.

The Eleventh Hour

The airframe failures related to spiral-dive situations more likely occur when the pilot recognizes the problem and begins to do something about it. The unusual attitude recovery drill in a high-airspeed situation is to level the wings and then correct the pitch attitude. When a spiral is perceived, either by reference to the instruments or by reference to the ground after spiraling out of cloud, the message is to correct the bank and pull out of the dive. Pulling out of the dive is likely to have emphasis, too, if the ground is near or if the altimeter is low and unwinding rapidly. This is where the airplane is usually broken. It could possibly even break itself.

Remember, the spiraling airplane is going much faster than the wings-level trim speed. Level the wings, and the airplane will zoom upward of its own accord, creating great stresses while seeking the trim status. Most pilots probably help, really hurt, the bad situation by pulling back on the wheel and adding even more stress to the airframe.

Tail Failure

On many aircraft, the horizontal tail is the first thing to fail. The download on this structure imposed by the upward deflected elevator in an attempted pullout can be extreme. Once part of the horizontal tail goes, other parts of the airframe follow.

Many airframe failures in flight occur when the aircraft is quite near the ground, meaning that the pilot perhaps recognized the inevitability of the situation and tried mightily to pull out of the dive. Even small deflections of any control impose greater than normal stresses at such high airspeeds, and in the case of a fully developed spiral, salvation might be found only by recognizing the situation while there is still plenty of altitude left and by adding a little forward pressure to the wheel as the wings are leveled to minimize the loads the airplane is naturally going to put on itself. The only chance for success in pulling out of a high-speed dive comes from doing it very gradually.

The airframe-failure accident's relationship to retractables does make a strong suggestion, too. When coming close to where this type of thing might occur—the prime risks are VFR pilots in IFR weather and any pilots close to thunderstorms—put the landing gear down. Flaps, even approach flaps, should not be used because the limit load factor is generally less when any flaps are used—meaning that it takes less g-load to overstress the wings.

One other item: When airframe failure in flight occurs in thunderstorm areas, the failure is usually preceded by a loss of control. It is rather rare for a failure to be documented that relates only to a catastrophic encounter with turbulence.

Doctors and Bonanzas

The doctors and their Bonanzas come up again at this point. It is true that Bonanzas have more airframe failures in flight than any other type. But it is also true that there are more Bonanzas in the fleet than any other retractable. During a two-year period, in fact, the Bonanza flew along with about the same airframe-failure rate as the other retractables, indicating that its pilots did well at staying out of spiral-dive situations. Then, in another year, the Bonanza's rate was substantially higher. In that year, though, the Bonanza's overall accident rate remained steady, about average when compared with the rest of the fleet.

Mooney

The Mooney is a retractable, yet it almost never shows up with an airframe failure in flight. Perhaps the simple, full-time, single-axis autopilot included as a standard lateral stabilization device on Mooneys for many years has had a role in this. Unfortunately, the Mooney's overall weather accident rate doesn't show a lot of benefit from its lack of involvement in airframe-failure accidents. Perhaps this indicates that if you save a pilot from one thing as he moves on into weather over his head, it only serves to postpone an inevitable sudden stop. Unhappy thought.

The important thing to remember when flying a Mooney or a fixed-gear airplane is that the relative immunity to airframe failure that seems to be offered doesn't mean anything. It is just as easy to lose control of one as another (except where the lateral stabilization device is considered). The fixed-gear airplanes have an accident type very similar to the retractables when a pilot loses control in weather: They hit the ground out of control, but whole. And in a high percentage of the airframe failures in retractables, the airplane would probably have struck the ground disastrously whether or not it failed.

Comparison?

In any study of accidents by make and model, there is an irresistible temptation to develop numbers on comparative accident rates. By so doing, one might imagine that it would be possible to show which airplanes do best and which do worst in the hands of average pilots doing average flying.

The development of truly meaningful numbers is elusive for several reasons. For one thing, the available information on the number of hours flown is approximate at best. For another, the samples are often small enough so that rather slight variations or strange sets of circumstances can create what appears to be a large problem.

Using FAA numbers on registered aircraft and their estimate of hours flown per aircraft in each class (single-engine, multiengine) and developing a fatal accident rate per 100,000 hours for each, airplanes with over 5,000 examples in the fleet show very little deviation from an average. In most cases, any deviation that does appear can be easily rationalized; i.e., a faster airplane might have a higher rate per hour that would come down to average if it were computed on a mileage basis. And airplanes that are used for recreational flying tend to trend on the high side because they are more often exposed to high-risk situations. The Cessna 150 and Piper PA–28 are a bit higher than the transportation-type airplanes, too, but they aren't markedly higher and their rate is almost identical in the year calculated.

Abnormalities

Moving into airplanes in lower numbers reveals some almost startling variations from the average, and it is here that one inclined to the sensational could try and pull a mangy rabbit from a hat to prove something. Behind numbers are facts, though, and careful study of each abnormal accident rate almost always indicates unusual circumstances.

Take the Cessna 421 and 414, for example. They are very similar airplanes. The 421 outnumbers the 414 in the fleet by a substantial margin, and yet in a recent year one 421 was involved in a fatal accident while *seven* 414s were involved in fatal accidents. The 421 involvement was an expected or slightly less than expected number; the 414 involvement was difficult to believe. The airplane's fatal accident rate for the year was something like 4½ times as high as the average for the general aviation fleet and from 8 to 10 times as high as the rate in business and corporate flying, where the 414 is most often used. The first thought was of a mistake, but a careful check indeed revealed seven 414 accidents.

Unrelated

The careful check also showed that not one of the accidents was directly related to the airplane's handling qualities or to its systems.

One 414 pilot descended into a mountain; improper IFR operation was given as the reason. That works in any airplane.

A 414 was destroyed when its pilot descended below the minimum descent altitude on a night, nonprecision approach. The pilot in command of this flight was in the right seat.

A pilot without an instrument rating was on top of an overcast at 19,000 feet in a 414. The overcast was entered for a descent, control of the airplane was lost, and the results were obvious.

Another pilot without an instrument rating continued VFR into IFR conditions in his 414 with disastrous results.

A pilot who had been denied a medical certificate flew a 414 into a mountain on a dark night.

A 414 pilot returning solo from a trip decided on some aerobatics in the traffic pattern. A stall followed a low-level roll.

And a private pilot stole a 414 and apparently crashed at sea.

There is only one airplane-connected item worthy of note in those seven accidents. The 414 is a basic pressurized twin. It often sells to people stepping up to that class airplane. Note that two of the accidents involved VFR pilots in IFR weather. It is safe to say that any combination of a pilot without an instrument rating and an airplane with the capability of the 414 is likely to be lethal. It is just not practical to extract transportation from *any* airplane without IFR capability, and the faster and higher the airplane flies, the more impractical and unsafe it becomes.

AA–1

One other airplane stands out as having a higher than average accident rate. It is the two-place AA–1 series, the Yankee and the Grumman American Trainer and Tr2. The airplane is not in the fleet in great numbers, but there are enough and there have been enough accidents to establish that its accident history is worth study.

The AA–1 has higher wing loading than other contemporary two-place airplanes. The airplane, especially the Yankee, also has brisk stall characteristics and was not approved for spins during the time of this accident study. (A program to approve the airplane for spins was active at the time this was written, but it will involve modification to the airplane.) The spin prohibition is emphasized with a placard on the instrument panel. It is a good training airplane in the sense that it is more demanding than others. A pilot who learns to fly in an AA–1 would probably find the transition to faster and heavier airplanes quite easy.

The accidents mirror the airplane's characteristics. About half tend to be of the stall/spin variety, often with the pilot looking for trouble. For example, an AA–1 was involved in a stall/spin accident following fuel exhaustion at night. Another came to stall/spin grief as a student pilot was doing low-level aerobatics. One AA–1 had a history of engine problems and gave up the ghost on takeoff, followed by a stall/spin accident. In another, a takeoff was attempted with fuel selector positioned on a dry tank, and a stall/spin accident was the result. A private pilot buzzed down the runway in an AA–1, pulled up steeply, and stalled. In another case, an AA–1 on a student solo flight spun to the ground.

Other fatal AA–1 accidents are of the type that happen to all airplanes: An overload on a short strip, fuel exhaustion, continued VFR into adverse weather, an attempted takeoff in a damaged airplane, a collision with a car, and a ground collision with another airplane are all on the list.

The AA–1 is a different airplane. It is a lively airplane to fly. It's even okay to fly it with the canopy opened. Its nature brings out the playfulness in some pilots, and this shows in the accident records.

Pilot Time in Type

There has to be a relationship between a pilot's flying time in an airplane and the risk involved in flying that airplane, but it might not be as significant as a lot of other factors.

Everyone starts out with zero hours in type, so that is an exposure for all pilots. And pilots with five or less hours in type do have some accidents, with about 5 percent of the fatals and total accidents accounted for by this group. Relative inexperience past that first five-hour hurdle is also a significant factor, with 11 percent of the fatal and 16 percent of the total accidents involving pilots with from six to twenty-five hours' flying time in the type of aircraft they wrecked.

This should make a strong suggestion about our approach to airplanes. The checkout is important and those first hours bear watching, but it is after we get a few hours under our belt that we are more likely to prang the bird. Perhaps by this time we feel there's nothing left to worry about.

A pilot's total experience in similar airplanes has a lot to do with capabilities in a given make and model, too. The Cessna 150, 172, and 182 all bear a resemblance, for example, with their high wings and big flaps. A pilot flying a 150 would step up to one of the bigger Cessnas with more grace than might be found when moving into another brand of airplane. Retractable-gear airplanes would all have to be more or less grouped, too. A pilot with 4 hours in a Bonanza as well as 4 total hours in retractables couldn't be considered as well-prepared as a pilot with 4 hours in a Bonanza and 500 hours in other retractables, for example.

The pilot's time in type does have a direct relationship with the type of accident. For example, when looking at the two most serious accident causes, weather and stall/spin, we see that pilots with less time in type than average have more stall/spin trouble than pilots with more experience in the airplane they are flying; whereas the pilots with more experience in type tend to run afoul of weather more often than pilots new to an airplane. Pilots also tend to have more than their share of trouble with systems, especially fuel systems, in their initial flying hours in an airplane. This is especially true in more complex airplanes.

There's little mystery to airplanes, though, and the record only suggests that a properly trained pilot can fly any airplane with an equal degree of safety. And for the airplane salesman who tries to use safety or who tries to link danger and a competitive product, a Bronx cheer.

11 | The Intrepid Airperson

All pilots have straight teeth and a crooked smile. All eat properly, none are fat, eyesight is crystal clear, and not one aviator misses daily exercise. The annual physical exam insures that everything is always 100 percent.

If all that were true, either everyone would want to become a pilot because of the health benefits, or few people could qualify to be a pilot. In real life the actual physical profile of pilots covers the spectrum, with the exception of those suffering from automatically disqualifying problems such as heart trouble and diabetes that can't be controlled by diet. In fact, only about 1 percent of the people taking FAA physicals fail. That shows that an average person does quite well. There is no substantial accident history related

189

to in-flight disability caused by health problems, too, so the criteria for medical certification must be more than adequate.

When a pilot does keel over at the controls, leaving a nonpilot to try and salvage the situation, it creates headlines. This might give the impression of a relatively frequent happening, but the record shows only a dozen or so annual cases of pilot incapacitation, and a substantial number of these are related to the monumental consumption of alcoholic beverages, which will be discussed in the next chapter.

From the Heart

True instances of airborne incapacitation are usually related to the heart and usually involve pilots in their forties. Some older, some younger, but the age number starts with a four in most of the cases. Perhaps this is evidence of a stressful time in the lives of the type of people who fly. Business and personal demands tend to peak at this time. Careers are cast in stone (or turned to sand), and kids go off to expensive colleges. The businessman-pilot probably pushes harder during these years than any other, taking a toll on the old pump. Maybe people who use airplanes push hardest of all, too. Use of the airplanes is certainly evidence of a desire to maximize effectiveness.

Still, incapacitation is not a large problem. Those who are concerned about it can obtain some peace of mind, too, by having frequent passengers understand the operation of radio and autopilot equipment along with the rudiments of flying. Cases have been recorded of completely inexperienced people landing complicated airplanes rather successfully, so the outcome isn't always bad even when the passenger has had no training.

Shoulder harnesses could be very helpful in more ways than one in case of pilot incapacitation. They can help soften the results of any impromptu flying performance on the part of a passenger, and if the disabled pilot has a harness on snugly, it would tend to keep him from falling into the controls. Unfortunately, the normally more desirable inertia-reel harnesses wouldn't serve the purpose of keeping an ailing pilot straight in the seat because they activate only on g-forces.

A couple of items for incapacitation: On-board oxygen might help in reviving someone, as might spirits of ammonia.

Carbon Monoxide

Carbon monoxide poisoning is an infrequent but possible cause of pilot incapacitation that affects passengers on an equal basis. This often comes from cabin heaters—either the exhaust muff heaters in single-engine airplanes or combustion heaters used in twins. If fumes are noticeable, if a headache develops, or if there's a giddy feeling, suspect carbon monoxide. The cure is to turn off the heater, open vents or a window, use oxygen if it is available, and, in the case of a suspected problem in a single, lean the mixture severely. Less carbon monoxide is produced at leaner mixtures. Carbon monoxide detectors are available, too, and a good preventive measure is to have the exhaust system carefully checked on a regular basis.

Basic Health

Even though it is not documented, the pilot's physical well-being probably figures in more accidents than the relatively few attributed to incapacitation or impairment for reasons other than alcohol. To contemplate these, we almost have to rely on imagination and personal experience. Anyone who has flown much has recognized a relationship between how a person feels and how a person flies, and if we recognize this relationship and work around it, minor things are less likely to cause problems.

Fatigue

Fatigue is probably the most frequently encountered problem. Professional pilots might not have this problem because operating the airplane is their job. They should reach the airplane rested and ready to work. Most of us, though, operate the airplane as an adjunct to work or play instead of as a primary activity. For example, we get up early and fly somewhere to work or to play all day, then we fly back. The morning flight might be at top efficiency, but the evening flight comes after mind and body have put in a full day.

Frequently, accident reports say that an accident was caused by pilot error—the hapless lad flew the whole thing into a mountain at night—when you just know that a bit more than that was involved. The pilot was probably tired and wanted very badly to get home. The obvious cause of the accident might have been the pilot flying into the mountain, but the causes behind the cause were physical and mental fatigue and the desire to get somewhere. Especially when an accident occurs at night, fatigue might be considered as a possible contributing factor.

Two things that minimize the effects of fatigue when flying after a hard day's work are oxygen and food—a lot of the former and a little of the latter. Oxygen has the capability of sharpening both night vision and the mind, and I've found it very beneficial to use oxygen at all altitudes when tired, especially at night. And don't go off hungry, but big meals seem best left until later, until after the flight. A person is less likely to doze off or become decidedly dull when lightly fed than when stuffed. Another effective fatigue fighter can be an unscheduled stop for a soda and a stretch. Those able to take catnaps might even get a short snooze on the airport couch during the course of a relatively short rest stop.

Noise

Noise is a big fatigue producer and one of the easiest to manage. Earplugs can make a loud prop airplane as quiet as a jet, and they cost very little. Wearing them during a long flight makes an appreciable difference in fatigue. It also helps prevent the hearing loss that plagues pilots who have spent many hours in noisy airplanes. Do you hear me?

Medicine

Much has been written about medicines and flying. As might be expected, "never" is the most frequent admonishment in connection with medication and flying. Certainly antihistamines do make some people drowsy, and no prescription drug should be taken before flying unless approved by the prescribing physician or preferably by an aviation medical examiner. But some physicians dispute the outright prohibition on flying after taking certain mild medications and say that it is okay for the pilot to fly as long as he feels unaffected by the medication. That might be okay for some but risky for anyone who is prone to engage in self-deception.

Other Factors

Things affecting the thought processes probably play an even larger role than actual physical health problems. It has been noted that people experience basic ups and downs, which can be related to airplane accidents. And it has long been held that people prone to do something untoward might be more likely to do so when the atmospheric pressure is low. So there might be a correlation between the thought processes leading to an accident in bad weather and low atmospheric pressure. The two usually go with each other.

Be Practical

It wouldn't be possible to make practical use of an airplane based on flying only when one feels at the crest of the mental and physical wave and when the atmospheric pressure is high. The saving graces are being able to recognize our less than optimum days and our ability to compensate for any weaknesses that develop. A methodical approach to flying is the best way to do this. We don't want to base aeronautical success on the fast thinking and perfect coordination that might come on our very best days. We should instead base success on procedures and flying techniques that withstand the tests of time and temperament. Then the good days will be just that much better. The same thing holds true for atmospheric pressure. The clear days with high pressure are the easiest anyway, and that is when we probably feel sharpest. On the grungy days, we might tend to match the sky with our mood, but the flying had best be according to a methodical plan that gets the proper things accomplished at the proper time.

Panic and Confusion

The self-discipline required to perform when not at peak is relatively easy to develop. In times of extreme stress, that self-discipline is more difficult to find. Search, though, because the outcome of some difficult situations is likely to hang on the pilot's ability to control himself as well as the airplane.

An example comes to mind. A private pilot without an instrument rating started out VFR but wound up flying in turbulent clouds. He made contact with stations on the ground and was doing a tolerable job of flying and maneuvering the airplane toward an airport, despite the fact that he was in a hostile environment. The pilot remained in control of the airplane and himself until the time of fuel exhaustion. Then the airplane was allowed to dive into the ground at high speed. Panic would have to be considered in this case. After an initial serious error, the pilot had been doing well at salvaging things until a climactic situation developed. The chips were down. An extremely difficult situation was at hand, and it had to be managed properly and immediately. Then he blew it. The airplane was lost, or given up, and nature took its course. If reason had prevailed, if the flaps had been lowered, and if the airplane had been slowed to a normal gliding speed, the impact might have been reasonably soft and the incident might have had a much happier ending.

Thunderstorms v. Thought Processes

Many of the airplanes lost in thunderstorm turbulence could also be related to a pilot not managing the required thought processes for survival.

A thunderstorm is a terrifying thing. The turbulence is severe, and the rain makes unbelievable noise. The airplane is difficult to control at best, and the overall impression is one of occupying a small space between a large rock and a very hard place. Some might give up the ship and accept whatever comes next.

I recall a letter from a pilot who lost control in a thunderstorm and spent several moments just contemplating his fate before taking some action. He felt doomed, and it took him a bit to convince himself that he might still have a chance. Then he pulled the throttle back, the airplane flew out the side of the storm, and he was able to recover and fly on. Others might keep trying, but worsen the predicament by doing the incorrect thing, by trying to turn around quickly and get out. Trying a steep turn in strong turbulence is a good way to lose control of an airplane. Still others seek to solve the problem with the radio. In a trying time, most pilots do have a tendency to use the radio in an attempt to talk their way out of a situation that really responds only to the pilot's mind, eye, and hand. The time for talk is before, when asking the questions necessary to locate and avoid the storms.

The ones most likely to succeed in an area of turbulence would be the ones who set the priorities and methodically work at them, despite the hostile environment. Certainly nobody but the pilot can fly the airplane in such a situation. The pilot who realizes that and scoots down in the seat under a tight belt and works as calmly as possible at keeping the attitude about level and the angle of bank as close to zero as possible has the best chance of emerging from the other side of a storm, battered but unscratched.

Any Time

Thunderstorms are just one example of an instance where a pilot's control of himself is a critical part of success. A forced landing or engine-out landing in a twin would also be a good example, as would the handling of an icing situation or any other possible but not normal situation. The decisions are critical in each case, as is the execution of the plan. The time allowed is often short, with few seconds available for procrastination.

Confidence

The role of confidence is a major one when a pilot is confronted with a difficult situation. Whether it be a thunderstorm, a forced landing, or whatever might come along, the pilot who feels confident that he can master the situation has a better chance of finishing things successfully. If overconfidence got the pilot there in the first place, that is bad, but if confidence can help the pilot think clearly and act intelligently in handling the airplane, that is good. However it works out, any pilot who is overwhelmed with the feeling of being a passenger, not in complete control of the flight, has a serious problem.

Oxygen

Moving back to keeping the body going, oxygen is the best thing we can buy to help our well-being while aloft. It is not only a good fatigue fighter, it can also become a necessary personal item before the regulations begin requiring it above 12,500 feet. There's no way a person who lives near sea level can fly all day at 10,000 feet and remain sharp for a demanding approach and landing at the end of a flight without using supplementary oxygen. It is good to have oxygen available on all long flights, regardless of the altitude, and it should be considered necessary for all operations above 10,000 feet. It is wise to lower that altitude at night.

Young and Old

Chronological age is considered by some to be a safety consideration, and there are some things in the record to suggest a relatively minor relationship between a pilot's age and the ability to operate airplanes safely. Whereas the nonfatal accidents tend to run in proportion to the number of pilots in any given age group, the total accidents don't quite conform to the pilot population.

The youngest pilots tend to do the best. The 16-to-19 age group has fatal accidents at a rate of about one-half the percentage of this group's representation in the total number of pilots. This is quite the opposite of their experience in automobiles.

Young pilots do well for a number of reasons. They learn fast, their reflexes are quick, and most have a lot of respect for airplanes. The young pilot is probably less prone to buzz or press on into weather. This is in contrast with the young automobile driver (possibly the same person) who might speed or otherwise operate an automobile in a reckless manner. Also, a high percentage of the pilots in this age group are student pilots, and students are subjected to more direct supervision. A substantial number of the young pilots who do have accidents tend to have at least a private certificate, which suggests that their record becomes more nearly average once they are out of the nest and off on their own.

Twenties

The 20- to 24-year-old pilots do well, too, but the best showing of all is in the 25-to-29 pilot group. This is the largest group numerically, and it is fairly evenly divided between student, private, and commercial pilots. If a figure were available on the average annual hours flown in relation to pilot age, I would guess that 25- to 29-year-olds would probably run average or a little above average, too. A lot of the active flight instructors are about this age, and they would balance any lower activity among students, who are more numerous than in the older pilot age brackets.

Pilots in their twenties probably do well for the same reasons as the teenagers. The sharp reflexes are still there, they catch on fast, and for some reason the young seem less prone to fly on into the face of obvious adversity.

Moving On

Once we move into our thirties and forties, we don't do as well. The 30- to 34-year-old pilots are slightly above the line in fatal accident involvement, and the peak is reached in the 35- to 39-year-old group. I did a similar study 11 years ago and found the same thing to be true. The 35-to-39 group had the worst record then, too. At that time, I offered the thought that these pilots were the ones who might have learned to fly right after World War II while in their early twenties, on the GI bill, and that the record might be a reflection on the quality of training during that period. If so, then the 45-to-49 age group should reflect this weakness in a study conducted 11 years later. It does to some extent, but it is not as far above average now as the 35-to-39 age group. So that might be considered an accident-prone period in the life of all pilots.

Why should people in their late thirties have more problems with airplanes than pilots of other ages? Nothing stands out when studying individual accident reports. The probable causes follow the averages. The percentage of students, private pilots, and commercial pilots involved is as might be anticipated: Not many students, a lot of private pilots, and a few commercial and ATRs were at the controls in a rather large sample of 35- to 39-year-old-pilot fatal accidents.

If one thing stands out, it is the quality of the airplanes that pilots in this age group destroy. It is good equipment. If the line is drawn right above the Cessna Skyhawk class of airplane, and all airplanes above that line are classified as high-performance airplanes, then almost 70 percent of the accidents involving 35- to 39-year-old pilots were in high-performance airplanes in the sample studied. This is perhaps an age where a person has had time to succeed and to afford the good things, and a time when that same person is more inclined to manage the risks of flying rather poorly.

Some 35- to 39-year-olds spin in, some descend into the ground on IFR approaches, some continue VFR into adverse conditions—it's all there, in both singles and twins. There's just more of it.

Over the Hill

Pilots in their forties also have more accidents than might be expected. They too have their accidents in rather nice airplanes, and there appears a discernible tendency of this group, especially the 40- to 44-year-old pilots, to have an above average number of weather-related accidents. The most common weather problems follow the familiar script of a private pilot without an instrument rating continuing VFR into adverse weather conditions.

When a pilot reaches forty, might he or she develop more of a "damn the torpedoes" outlook about weather and press on? Might we tend to develop a more overwhelming feeling about the importance of our presence in a given place at a given time and take more risks to achieve that goal? The record suggests that reaching this age doesn't have much influence on parting the clouds for a VFR flight, nor does any business or professional success on the ground. When at the controls of an airplane, a pilot is a pilot. What he or she does on the ground just doesn't count when flying.

Fifties

When in their fifties, pilots do a bit better, with the best record coming in the 55-to-59 age group. A very high percentage of the accidents involving pilots in their fifties are weather-related, which would be expected. At this age, the playfulness that might lead to buzzing should be gone, and there should be a level of maturity that would preclude doing other careless or reckless things with the airplane. It's too bad this couldn't carry through to the pilot's relationship with weather, but it doesn't.

Senior Pilots

The senior pilots, those over sixty, had more problems than I expected in this sample. The sample was enlarged to double-check this involvement because in the age/accident study done eleven years ago the senior-pilot involvement was just about average. Even with a much larger sample, the older pilots tended to be involved in fatal accidents more often than expected.

One thing did compromise this finding. A number of the pilots involved were exactly sixty. That would tend to reinforce the theory that age does not have a direct bearing on accidents: if those an even sixty were taken out of the sample, then the pilots sixty-one and older would have a record that is about average.

The senior pilots who have accidents do it in weather more often than not, and, as noted earlier, this age group does not figure in pilot incapacitation accidents in any abnormal number.

As Might Be Expected

In total, I think we find that all the aberrations in the record that can be related to physical well-being are logical. If a pilot is aware of them, they shouldn't cause trouble. Managing fatigue and not flying when ill or when under the influence of medicine is pure common sense. Being aware of the possibility of a carbon monoxide problem is quite simple. Use of supplementary oxygen at appropriate times is a reflection of basic wisdom.

Avoiding the risks generated by the mind is much more difficult. The thread here runs throughout the accident picture. In every area the failures generally have little to do with the pilot's physical abilities or the airplane. Perhaps we can do the most effective work by always flying on the basis of a self-challenge and -response system: "Is this a reasonable thing to do and the proper way to do it?" If the answer is always an unqualified "yes," then the risks are probably being managed rather well.

12 | Alcohol and Illegal Drugs

A high percentage of the pilots in our land probably enjoy a drink occasionally or even more often than that. And a high percentage of the pilots who drink operate automobiles after having consumed moderate amounts of alcohol. But most pilots abstain before flying. The rule says eight hours from bottle to throttle, and that rule is seldom broken. Why? Because it doesn't take much imagination to know that while there might be loving whiskey and fighting whiskey, laughing whiskey and crying whiskey, there just isn't any such thing as flying whiskey. Even the mild euphoria that comes from a couple of drinks can be all but debilitating in an airplane.

Of the small number of pilots who do try to mix alcohol and flying, a certain percentage might be reasonably successful. For example, I know one fellow who often has a drink before lunch or a beer with lunch, and then flies his airplane in the afternoon. He is in violation of the regulations, but he has no trouble and can see nothing wrong with his practice. And he may never have any trouble unless he changes the script. If one leads to two and two leads to three, then he might find the hand on the throttle overwhelmed by the bottle.

The Scope

The size of the drinking and flying problem might be outlined by the fact that just over 6 percent of the pilots flying airplanes involved in fatal accidents were deemed by the NTSB to be impaired or incapacitated by alcohol. The FAA has always suggested a somewhat greater alcohol involvement than has the NTSB. They consider any alcohol a factor, whereas NTSB usually considers it only when the level is consistent with that used by most states for classifying automobile drivers as intoxicated. In other words, you can break the FAA's eight-hour rule without the NTSB taking note. And it is safe to say that over 6 percent of the pilots involved in fatal accidents had some alcohol in them. I doubt that the figure would be a lot higher, though.

The nature of the alcohol-related accident appears easy to outline. Over 90 percent of the accidents are fatal. There just aren't really enough nonfatal alcohol-related accidents to bother with. Also consider the fact that fatal alcohol-related accidents tend to outnumber convictions for drunk flying by about 4:1, and the picture becomes quite clear: Those who are caught are more likely to be caught by the airplane than by the law. And when the airplane collects for the pilot's transgression, it does it with total vengeance.

One part of this picture probably isn't completely accurate. I can't quite buy the fact that alcohol-related accidents are more lethal than midair collisions or stall/spin accidents and doubt if they really are. Virtually all the fatal alcohol-related accidents are identified as such because, under the circumstances, the pilot is not in a position to avoid the check for alcohol that is part of the accident investigation procedure. But after a nonfatal accident, a pilot who has had a few drinks might very easily avoid a blood-alcohol or other incriminating test. Said another way, if you knock yourself off doing it, you are sure to get caught. If you survive, the chances of being caught diminish—for that outing, at least.

Suggestion

The nature of the flying and drinking accidents offers a strong suggestion on who is involved in this type of accident. Circumstances usually suggest that accidents are *not* caused by social drinkers flying an airplane after a drink before lunch or a normal ration of liquor during an evening cocktail hour.

The strong suggestion is that most pilots who have accidents after drinking must be people with quite a serious case of alcoholism. The amount of alcohol consumed and the fact that a lot of accidents happen in the daytime tend to confirm this. In some cases, there is plain evidence that an incapacitating amount of alcohol was consumed by the pilot in flight. The highest level I have seen on a report would have resulted from the pilot, a 200-pound man, drinking about a fifth of 100 proof in the hour before the accident.

In about 20 percent of the alcohol-related accidents, the airplane just flies into the ground or the trees. In many such cases, the alcohol level suggests that the pilot might not have seen the ground or trees coming or didn't comprehend or care.

The alcohol level in an ATR-rated pilot who flew a twin into some trees on final, for example, was enough to cause a substantial deterioration in all processes. If you weigh 160 pounds, toss off about *nine* ounces of 100 proof in short order and you'll get the point, or forget the point, or something. Anyway, that's about how much this pilot had on board.

Mission Impossible

In many cases, a drinking pilot seems to undertake a flight that he probably wouldn't touch when stone cold sober. There are some weather encounters in there, often at night, that involve a pilot without an instrument rating launching into a dense fog. All the other weather factors are on the list, but they are perhaps not quite as predominant as in accidents involving sober pilots. This is probably because the drinking pilot's mission is not as often related to transportation as the sober pilot's mission.

Lesh Go Buzzing

Buzzing and low-level aerobatics seem to be the most popular outlets for pilots who are under the influence. Almost a third of the accidents are related to such playfulness. Some of the lower alcohol levels appear rather frequently in this type of accident, too, but a few pilots end their careers while buzzing or doing aerobatics with a pretty good load of alcohol on board. For example, a student pilot who was about two-thirds of the way into a pint went out for a little buzzing. In a grand finale, the airplane was pulled up into a magnificent swoop. The airplane entered a spin and that was the end. Or a commercial pilot with a pretty substantial amount of liquor on board tried some low-level aerobatics and flew into a pole on a low pass.

Larcenous Liquor

There are also a few stolen aircraft in the picture, but not as many as I would have thought. Some people use liquor to screw up their courage, and I'd have thought that more of the alcohol-related accidents would involve a joyride in a stolen airplane.

Age and Machinery

Pilot age is an interesting thing to bring into the alcohol picture. Pilots under thirty have far less than what might be their expected share of the alcohol-related accidents, as do pilots over fifty. Those in their thirties and forties make up for the difference, with far more than their share of alcohol-related accidents. The airplanes wrecked by drinking pilots tend to be pretty new birds, too. There is a sprinkling of older airplanes, but most are contemporary, and most are basic two- and four-place airplanes. (There was one helicopter on the list. It would take a super lack of imagination to try and fly a helicopter while drunk.)

This is contrary to the situation in automobiles. Aground, the most likely participant in an alcohol-related accident is between twenty-five and thirty-five, single, and drives an older car.

The alcohol/age equation is another example of how younger pilots must tend to have more respect for airplanes. Whereas they are automotively reckless and prone to drink and drive with more gusto than the old bus can take, most must tend to put the prescribed time between bottle and airplane throttle.

By Certificate and Experience

The distribution of alcohol-related accidents by pilot certificate has few surprises. There are few students, which is a
reflection of the fact that students fly with more supervision. A student would not be likely to go to the airport
wearing a few drinks, and even if the student did, the instructor would not be likely to let that student go flying in
an airplane.

The experience level of the pilots is rather high, too.
Almost half the pilots had 500 hours or more.

Purpose of the Flight

In the course of one year, there was a single alcohol-related
accident during a flight for hire. It was an instructional dual
night flight with an inebriated flight instructor. A couple of
accidents happened on business flights, and the rest occurred during pleasure and personal transportation flights.
That is quite logical, and it perhaps dispels any thought that
the businessman pilot would be very prone to this type of
accident because of the alleged social pressures to imbibe
heavily for business reasons before lunch, for example.

Research

There has been a considerable amount of research done on the alcohol subject, both in laboratories and in airplanes, and the conclusion is always what anyone could have guessed before the project started: Alcohol does have a very detrimental affect on a person's ability to fly an airplane. Any person who both flies and uses alcohol, and has ever given a minute's thought to the possible consequences of mixing the two, could probably come up with conclusions similar to any research.

Some things—personal experiences, perhaps—might tend to lead a few people astray, though. Some often feel sharper after they have had, say, one drink or even a few drinks. What about that? Why not fly?

In research done a number of years ago, the FAA tested psychomotor coordination on some subjects through the use of light panels controlled by hand levers and foot pedals. As signal lights indicated different light arrangements, the test subjects used hand and foot controls to arrange lights on a panel as suggested by the signal. Alcohol level was adjusted upward with brandy and downward with time. Careful records of performance were kept, and the conclusion was that there was no severe deterioration in performance with blood-alcohol levels associated with a little less than two ounces of good liquor or a couple of beers for a 160-pound person. The effect of that amount of alcohol was about the same as the slowdown in processes induced by eating a big lunch. Past that level, performance deteriorated rapidly in the test subjects.

On the Other Hand . . .

If you like it, contradiction is available in any area subjected to testing processes: A study conducted by a foreign
air force offered a finding suggesting that alcohol doesn't
really affect performance. This program was conducted in a
simulator. The pilot flew a program sober, and then drank
half of a small bottle of gin and flew the program again. He
was in high spirits at this time, but did not appear intoxicated. After waiting a half hour, the pilot killed the bottle
of gin, washed it down with a pint of beer, and then headed
for the simulator again. He appeared intoxicated at this
time, though his mental processes seemed relatively intact.
After flying again, he slept for nine hours and then flew the
program one more time, fuzzy head and all. In measuring
his performance (in deviation from a ground track), they
found that the pilot didn't do as well when sober as after a
half bottle of gin. He improved even more after drinking
the rest of the gin and the beer. The worst performance was
the morning after.

That doesn't prove anything other than the fact that one
pilot did okay in a simulator after having quite a bit to
drink. It might, however, illustrate how some people lull
themselves into thinking that it is okay to fly after drinking.
Most of the pilots involved in alcohol-related accidents
have some level of dependence on alcohol, and they are the
type of people who search for reasons to justify the mixing
of alcohol with any activity. The fact that a pilot can fly in
a manner that seems satisfactory to him after consuming a
large amount of alcohol might just be the straw. That pilot

might indeed fly close to the line, but he might also fly into the ground while doing so. Or he might make an error in judgment that would result in a catastrophe.

Try It

If accident statistics and test results aren't enough, there is one thing the individual can do and one thing the individual can consider to prove that alcohol and airplanes don't mix. The thing to do is fly a simulator as you have a few. Fly the difficult problems. Fly the back course approaches and try partial panel: These are the things that make you think and reason as well as fly. Most any pilot will see a deterioration in ability.

Then consider all the letters you have written after having had a few drinks. Ever read them the next day before mailing them? Ever throw them away and start over? In an airplane you don't get to start over the next morning. The performance of the moment is the one that counts—no second chances.

How Much Distance?

There is no rational argument to offer in favor of flying while influenced by alcohol. The real question, for those

who both fly and drink, is in relation to the length of time
that should be put between flying and drinking. The hangover is the prime question.

Go back to the test with that pilot with a foreign air
force. His worst performance came the morning after the
night before. He could actually do a better job of tracking
while under the influence of quite a bit of alcohol than he
could when suffering from the aftereffects. If you had to
pick one condition or the other—under the influence or
hung over—does that mean that the pilot could do a more
effective job of operating an airplane safely while under the
influence of alcohol than he could later on? I think not. A
person might be able to command enough concentration to
fly a tracking maneuver reasonably well while inebriated,
but other things would likely be neglected. The reasoning
and judgment processes would be more affected while
under the direct influence than with a hangover.

Judgment is an important part of the alcohol v. flying
question, too. Remember that while some of the accidents
involve impairment or incapacitation in relatively normal
phases of flight, most involve difficult situations created by
the pilot, situations that probably would not have been
created by a sober pilot.

I think it questionable that a pilot's judgment would be
greatly affected by a hangover. If anything, the hangover
might cause more caution. It is just not an adventuresome
time in one's life, and certainly an airplane is not an attrac-
tive surrounding in which to nurse the ailment.

Lasting Effects

There are some demonstrable effects of a hangover that will affect the visual and vestibular systems, those most closely associated with disorientation, long after any measurable alcohol is gone from the system. These systems can actually show the effects of alcohol for as long as twenty-four hours. The phenomenon might not matter in flying where the tendency to become disoriented isn't strong, but a relatively inexperienced or rusty IFR pilot making a takeoff at minimums eight hours after having several drinks could have a battle on his hands even though no alcohol remained in the bloodstream.

Guidelines

The FAA's rule is that we not fly while under the influence of alcohol or within eight hours after the consumption of any alcoholic beverage. The eight-hour part is crystal clear, but it might mislead some by suggesting that eight hours is a good average time to put between the last drink and the airplane, regardless of circumstances. As noted, there can be some lingering effect that would make it unwise to undertake some flight operations eight hours after even moderate drinking. There are also situations in which a pilot might still be under the influence more than eight hours after taking the last drink.

Big Bottle

For example, consider a situation in which a 160-pound person consumes six drinks of 100 proof, 1 ½ ounces each, during a cocktail party that lasts from eight in the evening until midnight. That is quite a bit of alcohol, but spread over four hours after a heavy meal, it might not leave this person feeling that it had been a monumental drinking bout. And the person might feel it okay to go home, get some sleep, and fly at eight the next morning. It wouldn't be, though. There would still be measurable alcohol in the blood at eight the next morning. In fact, the alcohol wouldn't be metabolized until about ten.

At that point, at ten the next morning, it would be legal for the pilot to fly. But it might not be wise. Those who wish to guard against any hangover-induced hazard as well as the hazards of alcohol might well put eight hours between the time the alcohol is completely metabolized and flying. This isn't as restrictive as it might sound. For example, a 160-pound person can have three doubles (six ounces of 100 proof) between five and six in the evening and be eight hours on the other side at ten the next morning. If the takeoff is scheduled for seven, it would be best not to have doubles the evening before. If you don't want to fool with the mathematics, just abstain.

Math

If you do want to understand the mathematics, base your calculations on the fact that two beers or two ounces of 100 proof whiskey are metabolized by a 100-pound person in five hours. The relationship with weight is direct, so if you weigh 200 pounds, it'll take 2½ hours to metabolize two beers or two ounces of 100 proof. If you have four ounces and weigh 200, it'll take five hours. If you weigh 150 pounds and have two ounces, it'll take 3¾ hours. If you weigh 150 pounds and have four ounces, it'll take 7½ hours. It's all in direct proportion to body weight v. the amount of alcohol—100 pounds of body weight metabolizes two ounces of 100 proof or two beers every five hours. (If you drink 86 proof, you'll get rid of it in direct proportion to proof.) It should be noted that the alcohol in liquor consumed after eating is metabolized at a slower rate than the predinner, empty-stomach liquor. Its effects linger longer and are a good argument for skipping a nightcap the evening before a flight.

Alcohol v. Altitude

It is often noted that the effect of alcohol increases with altitude. I once wrote something that contained a contradictory note on this. It related a test in which people with no alcohol and people with enough alcohol to induce a moderate effect were taken to 12,000 feet. In the experiment the alcohol caused the same relative deterioration in performance in the alcohol and the nonalcohol group. The point was disputed by some physicians interested in aviation. It was their feeling that all factors associated with drinking—fatigue, hangovers, curative drugs, heavy smoking, and the alcohol itself—lower altitude tolerance. Perhaps the part about "relative deterioration'" is the key. The nonalcohol group started at sea level and suffered some deterioration, say, to eight on a scale of ten. The alcohol subjects didn't start at ten because of the alcohol. Perhaps they started at four and deteriorated to two. Each group might have dropped two points on a research scale, but the alcohol group might have gone from a coherent state to an incoherent state in so doing.

The argument about altitude is almost moot anyway. Most pilots who have accidents while under the influence don't fly at a high enough altitude for this to matter. It should be added, too, that oxygen is probably the best thing for freshening the mind when it's suspected that the effect of last evening's drink is making the morning fuzzy around the edges. Oxygen is much more effective than aspirin, and, in fact, aspirin increases a person's oxygen consumption and could contribute to lower altitude tolerance.

How Many

The accident record gives us a picture of the accidents caused by a pilot's excessive drinking. There's no way to develop a theory on the number of accidents in which low alcohol amounts or a hangover might be a factor, but there are bound to be a fair number of these. If there are as many such accidents as there are accidents in which the pilot is under the active influence of alcohol, as determined by the NTSB, then over 10 percent of the fatal accidents might be considered alcohol-related. That makes it a large problem, and one to avoid with understanding.

Marijuana and Friends

There is little in the available accident data to link the use of marijuana and other illegal drugs to flying. For one thing, marijuana is apparently not detectable in the blood test that is conducted during autopsies. Some drugs are, and they show up occasionally. The government, though, must not tend to put much effort into linking possible drug involvement with airplane accidents. At least I have one file in which an FAA-conducted toxicological examination revealed nothing of consequence, but the local coroner's report indicates drug levels compatible with impairment. Local people suggested that the pilot had a history of drug-related legal problems, but this obviously suggested nothing to the accident investigator.

Marijuana is the most widely used drug, and in visiting with some people likely to use it, I found a widespread feeling that there is probably very little flying done by people while under the influence of marijuana. It's just not that type of thing. Where liquor often tends to excite the adventuresome spirit in people, the effects of marijuana are more related to love and visions than to things like airplanes. Some suggested that the effects come and go in such a definite manner that you just wouldn't consider doing something like flying an airplane while under the influence. Of course, these people could be looking at the situation through rose-colored glasses, and at some point we could wind up with an identified drug/flying problem. There's no doubt that flying while under the influence of drugs would be as dangerous as flying while under the influence of alcohol, so the two activities must be separated.

The Deadly Side

There does exist a very hazardous identified relationship between marijuana and flying. A relatively substantial number of accidents occur as general aviation airplanes are used to haul marijuana into and around the country. Some are weather accidents, and some are prompted by fuel exhaustion. There almost seems to be a correlation between the Mexican border, the range of average airplanes, and the location of the fuel exhaustion accidents. They must strive for nonstop deliveries.

The stakes are high in this type of operation, and the accidents are examples of the ultimate in pressure flying. There could be more money riding on the successful delivery of an old Lockheed full of grass than on the average daily flights of a fleet of bizjets. The illegal nature of the flights would only tend to increase the pilot's eagerness to get it over with and to avoid any unscheduled stops. The pilots in such accidents tend to have a pocketful of licenses and a logbook full of flying time, but this doesn't seem to get the old birds through the weather and to the destination. Nor does it serve to keep the airplane flying after all the fuel is gone. In a way, it is a shame that such mishaps have to be counted as general aviation accidents. They have their effect on the total record, by which the activity is judged, even though the flights are conducted for illegal purposes.

Not Bad

I think the total record speaks rather well for people who fly. The involvement of alcohol and drugs in airplane accidents is clearly far less than is the case with automobiles, and we seem able to isolate most of the drinking and flying problems as ones related to people suffering from alcoholism.

As we manage our personal risks, this is an easy one to handle. Also, don't ever be reluctant to blow the whistle on someone you know who is unable to keep the alcohol or drugs separate from the airplane. It could be the greatest favor you might ever do for the person.

13 | Big Brother

In 1975 the FAA spent over fifty dollars for every hour that was flown by civil aircraft in the United States. The money was procured from Congress, largely in the name of safety, and it is only natural to devote some thought to the effectiveness of alleged safety-related services that exceed the operating cost of most airplanes in the fleet.

To begin with, the FAA is not entirely to blame for its enormous budget. True, the FAA begs, but only Congress can produce the money. It flows very freely after major catastrophes. The Grand Canyon collision between two airliners in 1956 prompted the first real opening of the gates. The public's fear of falling after a collision was excited: "Do something." All Congress knew to do was spend money. The FAA took the money and set out to avoid another Grand Canyon collision. They were successful; there hasn't been another case of two airliners colliding over the Grand Canyon—elsewhere, yes, but not there.

And so it has gone. Barn door after barn door has been closed after the horse has escaped. Airplanes have been certificated under rigorous government regulations only to develop flaws. Billions have been spent on the air traffic control system, yet there are still incidents and accidents within the system. Pilots have been burdened with more and more regulations and increased equipment requirements, yet they still fly airplanes into the ground. Each time some part of the system shows a weakness, the FAA is called on the carpet. Instant experts crawl out of the woodwork. Fingers are pointed, and finally something, anything, is done to close another barn door. If at any time Congress wanes in its enthusiasm for funding the FAA, you can almost imagine an empire builder there clandestinely approaching Senator Claghorn at a party: "Okay, Senator, don't give us the money we want. But next time you fly, you might die. Don't forget that."

That is probably the way it will continue, too. Congress will appropriate, the FAA will spend, and there will always be some risk in aviation. There is no way to remove it all. The exercise on collision avoidance systems is a good example. The FAA knows that there will always be some collisions. The only way to eliminate the collision risk would be to let just one airplane fly at a time. Congress knows this, too, but nobody in government will look the flying public right in the eye and tell the truth: If you can't accept some risk of collision or other catastrophe, it's best just not to fly. There is no way to make it perfectly safe, but political considerations cause our government and the segments of industry that feed off such things to live the lie of offering instant regulatory or electronic solutions to all problems. The public seems to like it.

The closest approach to absolute safety has been the space program, with a perfect in-flight record through 1976. Consider, though, the amount of money spent for each hour flown in space and the restrictions on the activity. It came to a bunch more than the fifty dollars per hour spent by the FAA, and very few people get to participate.

The System

Most of the FAA's safety effort is directed toward air carrier flying. The traffic control system consumes most of the money and is designed primarily to control airliners flying between large cities. It is both effective and necessary for them, and the airlines are slaves to the system. With few exceptions, they are not allowed to fly unless participating in the air traffic control system.

The general aviation part of the air traffic control system and our use of it are only by-products of something that was developed to suit the needs of air carriers. It works pretty well, but it isn't an integral part of general aviation's fiber.

The effect of the air traffic control system on the users was well illustrated when there was a labor dispute a few years

ago. The traffic control system's capacity was greatly reduced, and air carrier schedules turned to a shambles in
many parts of the country. They wisely flew only as air
traffic control service was available. General aviation managed quite well during the period, though, using a combination of VFR and IFR when available to get around. I think
we learned that while a complete shutdown of the traffic
control system would have an impact on general aviation, a
high percentage of operations could still be conducted safely.

Different Concepts

Air carrier and general aviation are simply different con-
cepts. The airlines are like railroads. Their activity is on a
schedule and is concentrated on routes between few airports. The aircraft and crews have a marked sameness.
General aviation is an almost entirely random operation. It
flies between 10,000 airports in all types of airplanes. The
pilots come in all levels of proficiency, from about zero up
to the equal of the best airline crews.

Whereas air carrier operations are adaptable to regulation and regimentation, general aviation is the type of activity that defies regulation and would suffocate under strict
regimentation. In fact, the only way the government might
truly be able to influence the general aviation safety record
is through restrictions. For example, we have continually
noted that the accident rate in pleasure flying is higher than
in business flying. The FAA might thus reason that it could

improve the overall safety record by promulgating regulations that would decrease the amount of pleasure flying.
Some of the ideas they have developed on mandatory
equipment requirements strongly suggest that such a policy
isn't foreign to the FAA's thinking.

The Best Example

The difficulty of regulating safety in general aviation is best
illustrated in the air taxi safety record. Air taxi has about
the same fatal accident rate as business flying, yet air taxi is
flown under much more stringent regulations.

Air taxi operators must have an FAA certificate plus an
operations manual. If flight plans are not filed, the operator
must have a procedure for locating the flight. Records must
be kept on each flight. A pilot training program must be
conducted, and detailed maintenance records must be kept.
None of that applies to a pilot flying for business reasons.

Air taxi airplanes must have 100-hour inspections,
whereas only annual inspections are required for business-
use aircraft.

Operationally, any private pilot can fly for business.
(Business flying is that not flown by professional flight
crews. Operations that utilize hired crews are classed as
corporate flying.) Air taxi pilot qualifications are much
more demanding. For example, air taxi operation at night
requires an instrument rating, and air taxi IFR operations
require a pilot with 1,200 hours flying time. Additionally,

either two pilots or an approved autopilot is required for IFR.

There are pages of regulations on things like instrument check requirements, weather, flight time limitations, engine-out performance requirements for twins, and restrictions on single-engine IFR flying. None of these rules applies to business flying.

The airplanes flown in the two uses are similar, the same really, yet the relatively unregulated businessman has as good a safety record flying these airplanes as does the much more tightly regulated professional pilot flying air taxi. If you want to jump up a notch and consider corporate flying, that done by hired pilots, its record is twice as good as air taxi, even though this flying is also subjected to much less regulation than air taxi.

More Is Better?

I suppose that a governmental answer to this will be even more regulation for air taxi operators. It probably will only serve to put some of them out of business, though, and probably will not help the safety record. In reality, the air taxi safety record is set by factors other than regulation. It is set by the type of operations and by the individual pilot's survival instincts. You could take the special rules for air taxi, wad them up, and toss them in the can, and the air taxi record probably wouldn't change appreciably. They would probably do as well operating under the same rules that apply to business and pleasure flying.

Thinking back to some of the accident causes does a lot to explain why excessive regulation doesn't do much for a general aviation activity such as air taxi flying.

Rules v. Weather

We noted that most of the IFR accidents involve premature arrivals—flight into the ground before reaching the airport on an IFR approach. Sure, there are rules on the subject, but the rules help only the pilot who wants to be helped. Those who wish to fudge can do so, often while almost convincing themselves that they aren't really doing anything wrong or illegal.

A lot of the night IFR accidents might not even involve a violation of any rule. In many the pilot's error is in succumbing to a visual illusion. No law against that. The pilot might properly stay at the minimum descent altitude until the runway lights or approach lights are in sight, and then fly into the ground while looking at these lights in the distance.

In other weather accidents, a pilot might start out with everything properly VFR for the flight only to encounter IFR conditions. At that time his brain, not a rule, will save the day.

Single-Engine, for Example

Then look at the FAA's restrictions on single-engine IFR operations by air taxi operators. It is so restricted that few operators bother even to try it. Yet the record in business flying, where single-engine airplanes are widely used for IFR flying, offers no reason for any curb on this type of activity. In a recent year, there was not one fatal engine-failure-related accident in single-engine airplanes used for business flying. You can almost sense the governmental reasoning behind a rule like this, though. Even if it involves no true and undue risk, an air taxi accident following an engine failure in a single could bring the ceiling down upon a bureaucrat's head. Have accidents in airplanes with two engines, though, and that can appear as "one of those things—we did our best on the rules."

When contemplating the regulation of air taxi flying, we can almost charge it all off as something that the FAA feels it must do in order to show an attempt at a higher level of safety where paying passengers are involved.

The Law v. Weather

Looking at the total picture, the problem of the pilot without an instrument rating proceeding VFR into adverse weather conditions appears one that might logically be expected to respond to regulation. The FAA is aware, too, that a substantial reduction in the number of this type of accident would lead to a marked improvement in the accident record, but so far they have not been able to develop anything of substance.

Some years ago, the FAA decided that limited instrument training for private pilots would help reduce weather accidents. The reasoning was that a pilot should at least have limited ability to fly by reference to the gauges so he could survive long enough to call for help, or to make a turn and fly back out of the inclement weather. The trouble is the smattering of instrument training doesn't stick unless the pilot follows a methodical proficiency maintenance program. What little ability is developed in the program tends to desert pilots when most needed. Also, it could have a negative effect by inducing weather-related boldness in certain pilots. There is nothing wrong with some instrument training for all private pilots, but I doubt if much value could be proven except in cases where the pilot moves on into real instrument training.

Minimums

The FAA has worked with some legal weather minimums in an effort to improve the situation. It abolished Special VFR at night, and this has probably prevented some accidents. However, only a small percentage of the airports are in control zones, where Special VFR is applicable, and pilots are free to fly VFR at night with one-mile visibility from any airport that doesn't have a control zone. So there are still plenty of legal opportunities for the pilot who wishes to tempt fate in the dark.

The night weather problem related to pilots on VFR flights might respond favorably to some adjustment in the regulations on minimum weather. Proportionately a very high percentage of the weather accidents occur at night. Going to the rules, we find that the Special VFR prohibition at night is *the only* regulation on VFR minimums that differentiates between daylight and dark. Certainly there is more than that to consider between day and night marginal VFR flying, and the FAA might eventually work in this fertile field. There's nothing wrong with night VFR, but logic certainly suggests that you need much better weather for it than for day VFR.

Day VFR

Whereas the FAA has never created even a mild rumble about adjusting the night VFR weather minimums, they have made noises about the overall VFR minimums. They generally meet with opposition from the users. The present minimums can be lethal in areas of rough terrain, but they do seem okay in flat country. Should the FAA place restrictions on the pilot flying in Kansas, which is flat as a billiard table, because people persist in flying into the relatively small but very adequate hills over in Arkansas? No way. The flexibility of VFR must remain, but we must do a better job of training pilots on the reasonable use of these minimums.

At an FAA/user meeting, one weather-related rule the FAA proposed to change was about IFR takeoff minimums. Air carrier and air taxi operations had takeoff minimums, but these did not apply to Part 91 operations, basically those not conducted for hire. This had been bothering the FAA for years, and they had unsuccessfully made the proposal to put Part 91 pilots under the takeoff minimum rule a number of times. This was another attempt.

There was discussion of the proposal, and finally the general aviation people in the audience started pressing the FAA for documentation, for solid reasons why the rule change should be made. Neither the FAA nor the National Transportation Safety Board had any justification to offer. Many logical reasons not to make the rule were offered, and finally an FAA person thought up one reason in favor: It would simplify the controller's lot by letting him deny takeoff clearances during periods of low visibility on a uniform basis. Hopefully, as regulatory changes are sought that will improve the safety record, the government will do better than that.

The Thunderstorm Rule

Thus far, the government has not made any rules about not flying through thunderstorms, even though the results of such an attempt are at times rather tragic. It has been contemplated, though, with the NTSB once suggesting that air traffic controllers be given the authority to deny takeoff or landing clearance when thunderstorms menace the airport, departure, or approach paths.

There is some logic to a thought like that, and perhaps it

would prevent accidents. Surely the local police have the authority to close a road that is inundated or otherwise affected, and this would only be an aeronautical parallel to such a rule. The rule could also cause chaos as airplanes of different weight and handling characteristics moved through an area of convective turbulence. If the controller were to be saddled with this authority and a Cessna Sky-hawk pilot reported severe turbulence on final, what would the controller do about the jumbo jet following along? If the airport were to be closed to the jumbo because of observed precipitation on radar and the Skyhawk pilot's report, the jumbo might be unnecessarily delayed. On the other hand, if the controller decided to factor the report for airplane size and let the jumbo keep on coming and it had an accident, then things would be bad indeed for that controller.

Thunderstorms are dynamic and rather unpredictable characters, and I suspect that they will forever defy regulation. Again, understanding is the key.

VFR Not Recommended

In another weather-related effort, the FAA instituted a program to make recommendations about not undertaking VFR flights. When the flight service station specialist deems that the weather is marginal or below VFR, the briefing is concluded with the statement "VFR not recommended."

Unless the pilots take it with understanding and a grain

of salt, this program could have a detrimental effect on safety for several reasons.

To begin with, if a pilot is deterred a few times, only to note that the weather was actually pretty good, that pilot is no longer likely to pay attention to any admonishment about weather from the FSS. And when a specialist does not say the magic words "VFR not recommended," a gullible pilot might take that as an indication that VFR *is* recommended by none other than the U. S. government. If the weather turns out to be bad, the pilot could be in for a rude awakening.

No-No

The FAA surely does have the wisdom to know that it can't solve the weather accident problem with rules and admonishments. The key is in pilot education and improved dissemination of weather information. Pilot education is the most important part, too, and the FAA actually took a step backward in this area not long ago with the institution of plain-language weather briefings. This is a real kindergarten delivery of weather information. Actually, the FAA should dispense only information and should work at developing an educational system that insures that every pilot knows as much or more about meteorology than the people now manning the flight service stations. The person flying the airplane is the person who must make the decisions.

Stall/Spin

There's no effective way to write a rule that would keep pilots from inadvertently stalling airplanes at the wrong time, so the FAA has had to rely on educational programs in working to reduce stall/spin accidents. In one way, this has taken on some aspects of a comic opera.

The FAA's flight instructor revalidation teams, groups that traveled the country conducting seminars, tended to reinvent the wheel occasionally. That was perhaps done in the rather common educator's effort to develop something tricky that can be used to show that the educator is smarter than the student. In one such move, they decided that when power is variable and available, the elevator *always* controls altitude and power always controls airspeed. Flight instructors sat through years of that, with the FAA people making snide remarks about people who disagreed. (Langewiesche, Kershner, and Collins were frequently mentioned.) The FAA stall recovery became a matter of putting the nose on the horizon with the elevator (hold altitude) and giving it full throttle (make airspeed).

Then, suddenly, the FAA changed, or at least it contradicted itself. An advisory circular appeared that plainly stated that the elevator controls airspeed and power controls altitude. Why the apparent change? Perhaps the FAA saw the light. The safety message for pilots is to carefully contemplate dramatic and controversial pronouncements on flying technique regardless of who makes them.

Proficiency

The FAA has done good work on writing rules to promote
pilot proficiency. The biennial flight review regulation en-
acted a few years ago has served to keep pilots in contact
with a flight instructor and to expose their skills to a critical
review every two years. This program has been exceptional
in excluding the government from the loop. The deal is
between the pilot and the instructor; the FAA has nothing
to do with the process.

The regulations on proficiency are good, too, and offer a
practical outline for a pilot to follow as a minimum. To
buttress its rule making on proficiency and safety awareness, the FAA developed an accident prevention program
that has been very effective.

The Ledger

The fact that aviation is more or less self-regulating is evident when the number of violations processed by the FAA
is compared with the total number of accidents. Accidents
tend to outnumber violations, and when you consider that a
lot of the violations are filed after a pilot has had an accident, it is even more evident that the airplane itself handles
a lot of the punishment. That isn't to belittle the FAA's
enforcement effort. They are alert and prosecute vigorously
when the occasion arises. Airplanes aren't like automobiles,
though, and many of the violations such as an inadvertent

entry into instrument conditions, come to a swift and accidental conclusion before a fed with a ticket book can enter
the picture.

Equipment

The feds require us to equip our airplanes with certain devices if we are to do certain things. Some of these requirements contribute to safety; others are more a form of
harassment. Encoding altimeters, for example, are devices
that make the airplane more compatible with the air traffic
control system, but their contribution to safety is not great.
In fact, if you consider the things that pilots buy volun-
tarily, those that are not required by law, such as DME,
autopilots, flight directors, redundant nav/com systems,
and weather radar systems, you will see that contribution to
safety by those items probably far outstrips the contribution
of the hardware items that are required or are being advanced as possible requirements to mesh with a complicated system of positive control of air traffic.

Big Money

In looking to prevent collisions through the imposition of
control and the spending of money, the FAA has long fa-

vored control towers. Indeed, a study revealed that relatively low-activity airports with control towers were virtually collision-free over a period of years. Thus, one might reason, the extension of control tower service should contribute to safety. How about a tower at the 840 uncontrolled airports in the United States that combine to account for two-thirds of all flight operations and 73 percent of the midair collisions? If experience is valid, it would cut the collision hazard at those airports, but the cost would be $17 million *for each collision prevented.* As we look toward solutions for safety problems, they must be affordable. There is certainly some question there.

So it seems that no matter what our government does through the FAA and through other agencies such as the NTSB, no breakthrough in general aviation safety is imminent or possible. And while a government role in aviation is very necessary, the record shows that this role could be diminished without any adverse effect on the safety potential of the activity.

14 | The Pilot/Airplane/ Accident Triangle

As we explore the accident record as well as history and the various things that are related to flying safely, it is continually noted that the pilot, the complex human, is the strength, the weakness, and the determiner of success. The federal aviation regulations recognize this with the following: "The pilot in command of an aircraft is directly responsible for, and is the final authority as to, the operation of that aircraft."

On the surface, it might appear that a person's behavioral traits in other areas could mirror the ability to accept that total responsibility and to manage risks in flying. It does not always work that way, though.

I know a lot of people who tend to drive recklessly: They speed, drive after having a bit much to drink, and generally

242 FLYING SAFELY

operate cars in an unsafe manner. But when near an airplane, their demeanor changes. The aeronautical operation becomes a calculated plot against risks. The planning is methodical and the decisions are conservative. The execution is precise. Not one corner is cut.

On the other hand, some people who are extremely cautious in their daily lives take chances in airplanes you almost wouldn't believe. They drive like little old ladies, eat health foods, go to the doctor at the first sign of a stomachache, and have a fire-detector system at home and life jackets for all on the boat. Aeronautically, though, they refuse to invest any money in proficiency flying, and they have the airplane maintained by the low bidder. They fly when fatigued, continually tempt the elements, and steadfastly refuse to get an instrument rating. They flaunt the proven trouble areas and generally use the airplane in a high-risk manner. Speak to such a person about this, and the response might come with a sneer, as if the pilot feels that nobody should question his right to kill himself in an airplane.

Responsibility and risk management in flying are very individual affairs that may or may not be affected by other things. Also, the responsibility part is often a difficult thing to grasp in a time when the government is trying to become a bigger factor in our lives. Some feel that they are provided with a GI umbrella and that there must either be no risk or that risk must be managed by government in every area. The politicians will continue to debate that in many relationships, but there is no debate in aviation. It is impossible to assume responsibility or manage aeronautical risks from afar. Flying is an individual, John Wayne activity.

What happens is determined by the pilot. If the pilot can't take the full responsibility, and cut it, trouble is bound to follow. Nobody can hold the pilot's hand. Nobody can fly the airplane for a pilot or cover up for any mistakes that are made by the pilot.

That all sounds a touch on the preachy side, but it is true, important, and the accident record provides an unlimited supply of examples to use in supporting the theory.

Weather

When checking weather, some pilots listen to a briefer, ask a few questions, and then take the product that someone else created in a few minutes and bet all the blue chips on it for hours. One such pilot said bitterly that there was no chance of thunderstorms mentioned in a weather briefing, yet he flew into a cell three hours later and had quite an interesting few minutes. The pilot criticized the person who gave him a weather briefing, but he should have looked into a mirror. The pilot should have continued checking the weather en route and continually reevaluated the decision to go. Any number of things would have informed him of the upcoming problem, but, no, he sat and waited for someone else to do his work, to tell him of the storm ahead.

Doomed from the Beginning

In many weather accidents, it is apparent that a pilot must have been driven into a precarious position by an almost blind obsession to get somewhere. This is illustrated in both VFR and IFR accidents. The pilot might continue VFR into adverse weather conditions, or, if IFR, might descend below an altitude in an attempt to fudge on minimums. These are highly individual deeds, prompted only by the pilot's personal devil-on-shoulder. They have to be the result of doing something without regard for the possible consequences.

As we critique our own flying, it is important to analyze all situations in which a decision might be influenced by other than aeronautical factors. For example, the desire to get back home from a trip, sometimes called "get-home-itis," is a strong influence that we should recognize. Personally, I have long noted that I am more prone to cancel the first leg of a trip, the outbound leg, than I am to cancel the last leg, the one that returns me to the warmth of my own fireplace. Perhaps there is a greater reward to returning home than there is to going away on a business trip, and I am willing to accept a bit more risk in return for the reward. I try to convince myself that isn't the case, that only aeronautical factors are considered, but when I look at the record, at the trips canceled over the years, I find some guilt.

A compulsion to get somewhere in the airplane is a frequent activator of the domino theory, too. Fly on to the destination even though the weather is perhaps below minimums. Then start the approach based on wishful thinking. Next, at the minimum descent altitude, descend an extra hundred feet, then another hundred. Maybe the domino crushes the airplane as a result of this transgression; maybe it doesn't. Even if it doesn't, a seed is planted: next time.

Determined Fellow, He Was . . .

A pilot with a fresh license illustrated the domino theory in action as he tried to shoot an instrument approach on a pleasure trip. The airplane and the situation were both a bit over the pilot's head, and the approach was missed even though the weather was quite a bit above minimums. Then, as the pilot came around to try again, the weather got a bit worse. The second approach was also missed, and even though there was some further deterioration in the weather, the pilot opted to try for a third approach. He flew into the ground on this one, and the cause was deemed to be a descent below the decision height without the runway in sight. That might fit the computer, but the cause was really the pilot's failure to recognize after two missed approaches, two chances, that he wasn't up to the situation. It was a personal decision that he had to make. Giving up meant that a rented airplane would have had to be flown back home and the rental paid without the mission being accomplished. So near, yet so far. Try again. Nothing in the rules against it. No help on the decision. Gamble and lose.

Limitations or Capabilities?

Some would suggest that this pilot didn't know his limitations. That is a bad choice of words, though, and when the preacher in a safety seminar pounds the podium, raises his voice, and says, "Know your limitations" with evangelistic fervor, I'm always tempted to ask where they are printed. On my Jockey shorts? An airplane's limitations are printed out in black and white, but people don't really have limitations. It is better to think in terms of capabilities: "I, as a pilot, am capable of shooting that ILS approach." Then, "I, as a pilot, just missed that ILS approach in above minimum conditions so I am apparently not capable of landing here today and had best go home, even though it means a lot of money for nothing."

Circumstances

Circumstances related to individuals are often closely related to accidents. And some things recur so frequently that we almost come to think of them as accident causes rather than circumstances surrounding the mishaps.

Flying for pleasure or personal transportation is a prime example of a circumstance that is strongly related to accidents. The record here is much worse, very much worse, than in business, corporate, instructional, air taxi, or agricultural flying. It only takes a little reflection to see why.

A person using an airplane for personal transportation

might be pressured to get back from a trip in time for work. Or there might be some reluctance to cancel for fear of losing face with family or friends. And often the pilot flying for personal reasons isn't as well trained as the pilot flying for business reasons. Nor might his airplane be as well equipped or maintained. The pleasure pilot pays for flying with after-tax dollars, which are a lot harder to come by than the before-tax dollars that the business user spends for his equipment, maintenance, proficiency flying, and perhaps even his training. Money can't buy safety, but at times failure to spend it can increase risk—especially in the training, proficiency, and maintenance areas.

Play

In local pleasure and recreational flying, we find many accidents that must be charged purely to playfulness on the part of an individual. Some can be charged to ignorance or poor technique, and many can be charged to showing off. There is a possible/impossible point in each and every thing that we do with airplanes, and the temptation to paw at the line between the two is strong when the airplane is being used to impress someone, to prove a point, or as an outlet for exhibitionism. To do these things is both fraught with peril and a highly individual decision.

Not Necessary

It shouldn't be necessary to accept an increase in risk based simply on the tax status of a flight—business or pleasure. However, there is plenty of experience in other areas to show that this is something that might be expected. In automobile accidents, for example, almost 30 percent of the people killed are between fifteen and twenty-four years old. That is an age when a car is more of an outlet, a toy, than a means to an end. Also, the automotive death rate is from two to three times higher at night, when the car is more often used for pleasure or personal transportation than for business and humdrum uses such as commuting and grocery shopping. Alcohol is a factor in about half the automobile accidents—a strong reason why the car is more lethal when used at night, for fun.

Do consider the automotive experience when reading of the relationship between pleasure and personal transportation uses and general aviation accidents. The higher accident rate that we see here must be a natural thing, based on individual behavior, and it might be expected in any activity. It in no way means that a pilot flying for pleasure cannot use an airplane as safely as the business pilot. It only means that the pleasure pilot must accept the same constraints that seem naturally to keep the business pilot from doing the things that involve high risk. Difficult, perhaps, and as individuals we'll probably never fly as safely when flying for fun as we do when droning along, straight and level, in hot pursuit of nothing more than the almighty dollar.

From the Start

Business or monkey business, there is often a clear relationship between an accident and the pilot's actions right before takeoff. Preflight covers a lot more territory than kicking the tires, squirting the sumps, checking the fuel and oil, and flying away. Those are the mechanical items; when realistic thought is not put into assessing the total picture, an accident can follow along very shortly.

This can be clearly illustrated when examining accidents related to weight, balance, and density altitude. The circumstances might put the pilot at a small airport on a hot day with a big load. That is, incidentally, a more frequent happening in pleasure flying than, for example, business flying, and the circumstances offer the pilot the opportunity of having one hell of a bad accident. Prevention would be found only in something the pilot might do *before* attempting the takeoff. Preflight action would be the only salvation.

Calculations might show that the takeoff would be impossible, at worst, or very close, at best. By making the calculations, the pilot would clear the first hurdle. The second hurdle would be recognition of the message. The third hurdle would be enough of a change in the circumstances to make the takeoff possible. Waiting until the cool of the late afternoon or morning might do it. Leaving some fuel out and planning a stop at the nearest large airport might do the trick. Wise pilots have been known to take passengers out of a small strip one at a time in a shuttle operation to a nearby larger airport. Then the whole group can fly together from that larger airport. Whatever is done is up to the pilot. Nobody is likely to make any suggestions or

offer any ideas. And if the pilot elects to try an impossible
mission, the passengers will probably go along.

Lots of Chances

Flying gives us a lot of chances, but we have to find and
take advantage of those chances. This is true in the mechanical sense as well as in areas affected by weather or
airplane performance.

Procrastination is probably the most common human
failure when it comes to mechanical items. I found a good
example of this when operating my Cessna Skyhawk, designed for 80-octane fuel, on low-lead 100-octane fuel,
which happened to be the only thing available to use. The
problems associated with using 100-octane fuel in 80-octane
engines were becoming legendary by the time my airplane
had 500 hours on it, and I had my first lesson at about that
time.

The airplane had just had a 100-hour inspection but was
not running as smoothly as it should. A fast check revealed
that the bottom spark plug in the number 4 cylinder was
terribly fouled. The shop put a new plug in and dismissed
the event with a "that-happens-all-the-time" attitude. I left
on a trip, and an hour into the flight the engine started
running rough again. The nearest airport was selected for a
landing, and there I met a more cautious mechanic. He
pulled the bottom plug from number 4, noted that it was
terribly fouled again, and said that the cylinder had best

come off to see what was causing the problem. It was full of lead deposits from the 100-octane fuel, and these deposits were breaking loose and fouling the bottom plug.

Short Memory

Only a few months later, I started having plug-fouling problems with the number 2 cylinder. In fact, it fouled both plugs once, and a four-cylinder engine running on three cylinders is on the far side of what you might call a rough running engine. It attracts attention in a hurry. And you would think that I would have learned by this time and would have promptly had the number 2 cylinder removed and checked for a cause. But, no, I convinced myself this was different, changed plugs, and kept on going. And I changed them again and again, and finally wised up and decided that the cylinder had to come off. I think I finally learned that when plugs foul once, be suspicious. When they foul twice, have the cylinder removed and checked to see what is going on.

The same requirement for basic suspicion of mechanical problems holds true in all areas. For example, I read of a pilot who had a great deal of difficulty starting one engine on a twin, but finally got it going and promptly taxied out and made an intersection takeoff. As the airplane was passing the end of the runway, the engine that had been reluctant to start decided to become temperamental again and it just quit cold. A very serious accident followed. If the pilot had been supersuspicious, he would have had the engine checked before the flight. Allowing for a normal amount of procrastination, one might have to let the pilot assume that the start was hard because of something like a vapor lock and that once the engine was running it would be okay. Even then, a mild suspicion probably would have saved the pilot by prompting him to start the takeoff from the end of the runway instead of from an intersection and to verify power output carefully before takeoff.

Pilot v. Type

Our relationship with different airplanes involves individual and responsible discipline because rules require a bare minimum in this area. For example, I stay legally current for passenger carrying in all prop single-engine land, single-engine sea, and prop-driven multiengine land airplanes weighing under 12,500 pounds simply by making three landings (or splashes, in the case of the seaplane) in any one example airplane in each of the three categories every ninety days. Three landings in a Cessna 150 and I'm current in a Bonanza; three in an Apache and I'm current in a King Air; three in a Lake Amphibian and I'm current in a Helio Courier on floats—legally current, that is (as the rules were written in 1976), and as has been noted before, all that's legal isn't safe.

While we might look at a checkout or practice some flying in an airplane before leaving on a trip as an admission of a lack of skill or proficiency, the checkout and some practice go hand in hand with flying safely.

There are numerous ways to delude ourselves as we fly different airplanes, too. For example, a pilot with instrument, single, and multiengine ratings is free to fly IFR in both single and multiengine airplanes. And I've seen pilots get their instrument rating in a single-engine airplane "because it is easier" and then attempt IFR operations in a twin without any additional practice or training. There is a risk involved in multiengine IFR flying by a pilot with only single-engine IFR experience, and accidents and incidents prove this quite frequently. There's more to distract in the twin, and a pilot should be trained and current on handling the distractions while operating in the IFR environment.

Burgeoning Question

As a result of some pertinent accidents, there has been a lot of talk about who is really responsible for qualifying the pilots who fly different airplanes. An incident I overheard on an air traffic control frequency outlines the problem.

The pilot was flying a Cessna 340, and when he first called the center to air-file an IFR flight plan, he identified his point of departure as a small resort area sod strip with which I was familiar. The strip is about 3,000 feet long, and the day was a hot one. As the pilot filed his flight plan, the fuel and number of people on board strongly suggested that the airplane was at or over gross weight when it left the small sod strip. I only wondered if he understood the risk involved in operating a twin in such a manner. Strike one.

As the pilot continued, there was a great deal of hesitation in his approach to the situation and quite a bit of misunderstanding between the pilot and the controller. The weakness was all on the part of the pilot. He read a clearance back incorrectly and then changed altitude after asking for a change, but before being cleared for the change by the controller. Strike two.

Then the inevitable thunderstorms lined up across the pilot's path. The airplane had weather radar on board, but the pilot was clearly not trained in its use. As the storms were approached, the pilot's continuing requests for information turned into plaintive pleading: "Please lead me through." It was a sad, pitiful exercise. It was quite obvious that while the pilot might have been capable of taking off and landing the 340, he was certainly not qualified to operate the airplane as it was meant to be operated. He seemed to survive that day's activity, probably with the help of an autopilot, but another day might well get him.

Whose Fault?

Who is responsible for a situation like that? The airframe manufacturer? The airplane salesman? The FAA? The insurance company? They all have a role in putting the pilot in the left front seat of the airplane, but the pilot alone has to bear the responsibility of operating the airplane, so it stands to reason that the pilot should assure that he is capable of doing so. The man had to have enough sense to make the money to buy the airplane, so surely it would be reasonably easy to convince him that it takes more than the legal (or insurance company) minimum to fly the airplane without wiping himself and his family out in one stroke. Aviation suffers through a lot of tragedies caused by situations like this; a substantial number of them are very predictable, and the solution is going to have to be found in individual understanding of the risks involved.

Not Compatible

It is true, too, that some people probably are just not compatible with airplanes. It is hard to tell an intelligent person that he or she should just push off from an activity like flying, but it occasionally needs to be done. Just as every person in the world is not cut out to be a doctor, lawyer, politician, or great lover, every person in the world is not cut out to be an airplane pilot. And when a person who doesn't adapt keeps trying, the result is frustration at best and an accident at worst.

How can you tell when a person should quit trying to master the airplane? The answer is both difficult and a highly individual matter. I recall one person I was trying to teach to fly a number of years ago and the mental torment the man was subjecting himself to while trying to learn to fly. Landings were seemingly beyond his grasp. Try as he would, he couldn't find the ground with the little airplane after twenty-five hours of dual. He would end each flight in a fit of frustration and vow never to come back. Then, in a few days, he would call for another lesson and we would try again.

Late one day when the air was smooth and hardly a breath of wind was stirring, he finally produced a string of reasonable landings. I seized the opportunity and told him this was it—first solo. I left him alone in the airplane and walked over to the side of the runway. He took off without hesitation, flew the pattern, and then made a successful if not smooth landing. The fellow refused to shoot another solo landing, though. In fact, to my knowledge he never flew an airplane again. He had soloed, and he left happy. I was glad that I had been able to solo him and was relieved that he quit flying because he would have always been a marginal pilot.

I've often thought about that person and have tried to develop a mental picture of a personality that would lead to such a problem. He was a smart guy, and the only characteristic I could isolate had to do with his inability to think rapidly and then make his hands and feet do the required work. His decisions were usually good, he could usually tell me what he had done incorrectly, but he was incapable of patching things up with his own hand. I guess he was a procrastinator in all things, and procrastination doesn't have much of a role in landing airplanes.

Methodical and Current

Once we are up to speed in airplanes in general and one airplane in particular, a methodical approach to flying remains quite important. I got a reminder of this when flying a rather sophisticated airplane with another pilot recently. We had flown the airplane earlier and were headed out for another round. The weather was quite bad, with rain and thundershowers throughout the area. The clearance finally came through, and when it did I ran my mental "instruments, controls, fuel, and trim" checklist, pulled out on the runway, and launched.

We had been off and climbing for about five minutes when the other pilot looked over to my side and said, "I guess we should have those alternators on." In our preoccupation with getting started, watching the weather, and getting a clearance, we had missed that part of the checklist. The embarrassing thing was the annunciator panel: Two bright lights were telling us that the alternators were not on all the while, and neither of us noticed them.

Practice Makes, Well . . .

Practice is an important part of flying safely. Oh, I don't mean that we should go out and practice chandelles, S-turns, and other such basic training maneuvers. Instead, we should practice things that are difficult, that require precision, and that are practical. An IFR favorite of mine is partial panel under the hood. Covering the artificial horizon and direction gyro simulates a failure of the vacuum system—a very real possibility—and the challenge is to shoot an ILS approach to minimums with things in this state. It's hard work, it takes some practice to stay current, but it is rewarding in the sense that it offers in my single-engine airplane the redundancy that I might get from dual vacuum pumps in a twin. I also like to practice spot landings. It's surprising how widely you miss the mark when rusty on these, and, again, skill at spot landings offers a form of redundancy. Engines seldom quit, but if one ever did, the ability to put the airplane precisely where you want it would be quite handy.

It is often tempting to practice only the things that we do well, but the opposite is much more useful. Practicing to learn something contributes a lot more to flying safely than practicing to exhibit perfection. And practicing is a highly individual mater. We set the time, the place, and the format.

Double Reverse

It was noted earlier that airplanes don't do well at keeping secrets. There are instances, though, where something that is not apparent can surface as pilots adjust to a new airplane coming into the fleet. Such situations are worth exploring because, in retrospect, a modicum of logic and reason might have prevented a lot of trouble.

The Twin Comanche example that was noted is a classic example of this. People buy and use light twins because they feel there is a safety advantage to be derived from two engines, yet a lot of Twin Comanche accidents were related to the twin-engine nature of the airplane. The airplane was the lowest-cost twin available, so flight schools and users trading up from singles were attracted to it. But the safety potential was apparently negated in the first years of use as asymmetric thrust got the best of people in training as well as in bona fide engine-out situations. The people using the airplane and the FAA just did not approach the situation logically, and the Twin Comanche's strength became a weakness.

The training part of this is an example of how pilots should recognize that there are instances in which we can't bite the apple at all. In flying at slow speed on one engine, things might appear okay, not squirrelly, until the moment the airplane stalls. The entry into an asymmetric thrust-induced stall would be very quick; one second the pilot might be satisfied with the situation, the next second he might be in an extremely precarious predicament. If at low altitude, there would probably be no hope for recovery; if at a reasonable altitude, recovery would be possible only if proper action were to be taken very quickly.

The individual has to protect himself through avoidance of situations like that. Some highly proficient multiengine instructors were lost in accidents of this type, which is a good illustration of the fact that abstention is the *only* form of proficiency in some instances. I don't mind poking around on the tender spots of a twin, but give me more than a mile of altitude to use in case it wants to wrestle.

Landing

The Twin Comanche has had another interesting experience that illustrates a further point. The airplane isn't one
of the most satisfying in the world to land. It tends to hit
level, regardless of a pilot's effort to make a tail-low landing, and ground contact is often with a very resounding
thud. New and old Twin Comanche pilots shared the bad
landings in the airplanes. I flew one for four years and
never learned to make consistently good landings. And my
definition of a good landing was one in which the tow bar
was not jarred from its clip-type holder at the roof of the
baggage compartment.

Despite the fact that the Twin Comanche was (and is) a
bear to land, the airplane never had any abnormal landing
accident history. Perhaps this suggests that an obvious
characteristic, such as an open challenge to the pilot on
every landing, might at times be less likely to cause real
trouble than a conceptual area such as multiengine.

Strapped

The pilot's approach to handling qualities does not have a
monopoly on determining safety potential. Hardware
counts, too, and shoulder-harness systems in airplanes are
highly individual items that can have a dramatic effect on
aviation safety.

Like so many people, I rather shunned the use of harnesses for years. I'd leave them stowed (if the airplane was even equipped), and if the airplane was harnessless I never gave it a second thought. I suppose that the rationale was based on ego: I would protect myself against any potential sudden stop with a perfectly timed burst of brilliance. Then I was awakened from that dream by a flight surgeon at a safety meeting. He made the flat statement that 25 percent of the people who died in general aviation accidents would probably have survived if they had been wearing shoulder harnesses.

He was a man of more than words. There were also pictures, bloody awful pictures of corpses that were used to prove the point. I'll always remember one of a young pilot, a friend of a friend of mine, who looked in perfect shape except for a place on his head where contact was made with a windshield-mounted compass in a relatively minor accident. A shoulder harness would have prevented that.

I was sold. I was later to be further sold by a movie made by an airframe manufacturer. They crashed an airplane with two instrumented dummies aboard into a dirt bank at fifty knots in an experiment to test effectiveness of the restraint systems. The movie was a close-up of the cockpit at impact. One dummy had the shoulder harness on and probably survived. There was no question that the dummy without a harness was in much worse shape. Finally, the good experience with shoulder harnesses in agricultural aviation finished the sales job.

Spin In

Back to flying technique, where there are a lot of stall/spin accidents in which the individual clearly loads himself into the boat. Recently a couple of very experienced professional pilots flying a rather old two-place airplane provided a perfect illustration of this. Witnesses reported that the airplane zoomed up from behind the trees, stalled, and spun to the ground. Someone remarked that the pilot had been flying the little airplane like that since acquiring it and added that he'd been wondering when he would cash in. It finally happened, as was probably inevitable. Hopefully, the individual at least had enough sense to know that the fates were being sorely tempted, and in those last seconds he realized that the upcoming sudden stop was a creation of his own hand. When it was too late, it was too late. The deed was done, and the pilot's alleged skill or proficiency could in no way change the conclusion made inevitable by one sweeping stroke of bad judgment.

With such an accident in mind, the primary conclusion of any study of the relationship between the pilot and the airplane is that there is little mystery to general aviation accidents. They most frequently happen when a pilot pushes too far or attempts operation on the far side of individual ability, airplane performance, or structural limitations. And the total product of all this is applied to the number of hours flown to become the safety record.

How Safe?

How is our safety record? How do we do when applied to the airplane in the real world?

For a benchmark, the crews of American Airlines recently flew more than 6 million hours between fatal accidents. That is probably the best safety record in the history of public or private transportation, whether considered in terms of hours, passengers carried, or passenger miles operated. Compared with general aviation's rate of one fatal accident for every 45,000 hours of operation, the American Airlines record is nothing short of magnificent. On an hourly basis, it is 133 times better; per mile, the figure would be even higher.

While general aviation in total doesn't do well by comparison with such a record, this in no way suggests that general aviation flying is inherently more dangerous than the flying done by American. No way. It is true that they do have performance advantages in their airplanes plus redundant systems and redundant crews, but general aviation also has some advantages. Our airplanes are simpler; if we do have a mishap it is at a slower speed with less aluminum to stop; and the majority of our operations are at airports where there is a tremendous margin built into the runway available. If they do have an equipment advantage, it is small—I'd arbitrarily say 5 or 10 percent. The real key to flying safely is in the way they operate their airplanes. The crews understand the risks, and they methodically fly in a manner that minimizes these risks. We can do the same thing. Flying any kind of airplane is just as safe as the pilot wants it to be.

Epilogue

In learning to fly, we accentuate the positive. We are learning to *do* something, to fly. In studying accidents, though, it is often obvious that the pilot might have erred more in the sense of doing something he shouldn't do rather than in the sense of doing something improperly. I thus thought that it would be worthwhile to offer a list of things *not* to do in an airplane. I do not offer this list as a course in how not to fly or as a complete list of things to avoid. Rather, it includes the most common items, based on accident reports, covering a great majority of the serious accidents. Feel free to add anything to it that you wish.

- Don't skimp on preflight duties. Check the weather and the airplane carefully.

- Don't fly VFR-day when the visibility is less than three miles and the ceiling is less than 1,000 feet above the highest obstacle within five miles of the flight path.
- Don't fly VFR-night when the visibility is less than five miles and the ceiling is less than 2,000 feet above the highest obstacle within five miles of the flight path.
- Don't make any exceptions to the first two rules and resolve to land at the nearest airport when either rule appears in danger of being compromised.
- Don't fail to check the weather when en route. Once every hour is a good practice.
- When IFR, don't leave the minimum descent altitude or the decision height until the runway is in sight. At night the rule is based on the runway lights. The approach lights do not count, day or night. They are to lead you to the runway, not to provide vertical guidance.
- Don't fly with a disregard for ice and thunderstorms. Given the right circumstances, either can easily prevail.
- Don't forget that you must fly the next mile before earning the right to fly the ones after it.
- Don't buzz or otherwise use an airplane as an outlet for exhibitionism.
- Don't fail to understand the importance of angle of attack and its relationship to the stall.
- Don't fail to recognize the possible need for reducing the angle of attack when considerable back pressure is being held on the wheel or stick during low-alti-

tude maneuvers or when excessive aileron is being held in the direction opposite the turn to prevent overbanking.

- Don't make downwind turns when speed or climb gradient is critical.
- Don't fail to ascertain that there is ample runway for a safe departure before every takeoff. This means careful calculations if there is any doubt.
- Don't hesitate to reduce the load when flying from small airports or in high-density altitude conditions.
- Don't overload an airplane under any circumstances, and check the center of gravity as within limits for every flight.
- Don't plan to land with less than one hour's fuel in the tanks.
- Don't forget that a midair collision can spoil your whole day. Look for, see, and avoid other traffic.
- Don't forget the principles of wake turbulence avoidance.
- Don't let anyone enter or leave your airplane when the engine is running.
- Don't forget to extend the landing gear of a retractable before each and every landing.
- Don't fail to get a good checkout in each make and model airplane flown.
- Don't explore any maneuvers that are not approved in the airplane being flown.
- Don't fly above 10,000 feet without supplementary oxygen.
- Don't fly when fatigued or ill.
- Don't fly when under the influence of alcohol or

drugs—either the direct or the lingering influence.

- Don't rely on anyone else for the successful completion of a flight. The pilot in command is solely responsible—in a practical, legal, and absolute sense.
- Don't fail to practice the things that can help you fly more safely.
- Don't fail to use a checklist for all operations. Do it all, every time.
- Don't fail to wear a shoulder harness.
- Don't ever base a "go" (or "keep going") decision on anything other than aeronautical factors. Business or personal considerations are secondary when flying.
- Don't ever fly with the thought *I think I can make it.* If you aren't sure, don't go.

Index

Headwinds, 62
Helicopters, 121–2, 126, 211
High temperatures, 112
Holidays and weekends, 43
Homebuilts, 135, 141, 143

Ice and icing accidents, 18, 19–24; geography of, 23–4; pilot's skill and, 21–2; twins v. singles in, 22–3
IFR. *See* Instrument flying (IFR)
Illinois, 119
Inertia-reel harnesses, 191
Instructional flying, 42, 171; engine failures, 143–4. *See also* Training
Instructors, 6, 168, 201, 237. *See also* Instructional flying; Training
Instrument flying (IFR), 2–3, 4, 17–36, 39, 184, 185, 253; accidents, 17–36, 177, 230; air taxi, 228–9; approach and landing, 33–6, 45–7, 57; compared to VFR, 17–18; control loss, 13; ice conditions, 19–24; night flying, 43–8, 49; pilots, 16, 21–2, 25, 28, 30, 44, 49, 244; rating for, 9, 184; risk, 17, 36; takeoff minimums, 233–4; thunderstorms, 24–31; by VFR pilots, 9, 11, 14–15

J-3 Cubs, 156
Jets, 127–8

Kansas, 58, 233
Kershner, 237

Landing and landing accidents, 21, 71–80, 159–64, 260; approach speed, 72–3; attitude, 162; forced, 53, 54, 58–9, 88,
138, 145, 198; gear-up, 162–4; late go-around, 76; overshot turn, 72; sheared on approach, 77–80; tricycle-gear airplane, 73–5; wheelbarrowing, 74–6. *See also* Approach
Landing gear, 148, 180
Landing speed, 144
Langewiesche, 237
Law, 16
Lights, 59; night landing, 46–7
Loss of control, 9, 12–15, 180; preliminaries, 14–15; in thunder storms, 25–6
Luscombes, 136, 167, 168

Maintenance, 152, 155, 167, 228
Maintenance areas, 247
Maneuvering speed, 70
Marijuana, 221–3
Mechanical failure, 130, 154–5, 250–2; propellers, 152. *See also* Engine failure
Medicine, 194, 205
Midair collisions, 115–29, 208; airplane types in, 118; avoidance measures, 125–9; at controlled airports, 120, 125, 128–129; final approach, 123; with helicopters, 121–2, 126; high-altitude, 123; high wing or low, 117–18, 121; military v. civil, 122; most hazardous times, 127; pattern, 116–17, 121; pilot's role, 121–2, 125–126; survival rate, 116; traffic density factor, 119–20; at uncontrolled airports, 119–20, 123, 128–9
Military jet accidents, 122
Minimum descent altitude, 35, 46, 49, 184, 245
MITRE Corporation, 119

Weather accidents (*Cont.*)
pilot's role in, 243–4; by plane type, 176–80; regulations and, 230, 231–6; spiral dives, 178–9; statistics, 10; thunderstorms, 24–30; training factors, 5–6; VFR, 1–16
Weather research, 28
Weight, 100–14, 147, 249; center of gravity and, 105, 108–10; density altitude, 110–11; distribution, 73–5; flying technique and, 114; maneuvering speed and, 30–1; rate of climb and, 106–7; structure and, 107
Wheelbarrowing, 74–6
Wheel landing, 75
Wind, 61–80, 82, 160; amount

of, 62–3; approach speed and, 72–3; departure accidents and, 63–4; downdrafts, 70; downwind turn, 65–8; effect of, 63–4; en route, 69–70; forecast, 69; landing accidents and, 71–80; over mountains, 111; upwind turns, 69–70; variable and gusty, 64–5
Windows, 126
Wind shear, 77–80; defined, 62; recognizing, 79–80
Wings, 31

Yankee, 185
Yaw, 92, 95–6, 97

Zoom, 89–90